A
MOMENT
IN TIME

Where Accidents
Become Opportunities

LORI GIESEY

Saved By Story

A Moment in Time
Where Accidents Become Opportunities

Published by
Saved By Story Publishing
Second Edition
Prescott, Arizona

Cover Design by Alyssa Coelho
Interior Design by Dawn Teagarden

Disclaimer: The Publisher and the Author do not guarantee that anyone following the techniques, suggestions, tips, ideas or strategies will become successful. The advice and strategies contained herein may not be suitable for every situation. The Publisher and Author shall have neither liability nor responsibility to anyone with respect to any loss or damage caused, or alleged to be caused, directly or indirectly by the information in this book. Written permission has been obtained to share the identity of each real individual named in this book.

Any citations or a potential source of information from other organizations or websites given herein does not mean that the Author or Publisher endorses the information/content the website or organization provides or recommendations it may make. It is the readers' responsibility to do their own due diligence when researching information. Also, websites listed or referenced herein may have changed or disappeared from the time that this work was created and the time that it is read.

ISBN: 978-1-961336-17-9 (paperback)

Printed in the United States of America

WHAT READERS ARE SAYING

"In the darkest hours, we are presented with the opportunity to face our greatest fears, insecurities, and demons. Lori's journey of loss, vulnerability, and ultimate courage is a testament to faith, love, and the human spirit. For anyone who has had to face their greatest fears, this is a great story of resilience and also one of unconditional love from the man who chose to stand by her, and for her—her husband Mike!"

Phil Black, Founder and Co-Creator of
The Accelerated Leadership Academy and Mastery

"Lori lives her life with such grit and motivation. She is a powerful depiction of how anyone can overcome odds by demonstrating resilience, strength, and the capacity to conquer battles within oneself. She showcases the desire to live a life she wants despite roadblocks in her path! This book will leave you inspired while also allowing you to see there's always an avenue toward your own goals and purpose in life!"

Master Sergeant Jennifer Sauer,
Security Forces, Colorado Air National Guard

"Several years ago, I encouraged Lori to tell her story! Little did I know that I only knew part of it. After seeing and hearing everything that Lori has been through, I believe if you set your mind to do something, anything is possible! You must first believe in yourself, have a great group of people in your life, and most of all have Jesus Christ as the center of your life. I believe Lori has all of this in her life, and this makes her an amazing person that I get to call my friend. I think you will find this lady and her story very inspiring. Thank you, Lori, for being part of my journey!"

Brandon Hall, D.C, Loveland Chiropractic

"What an inspiring story of Lori's journey from debilitating pain to robust health! She relates the obstacles she had to overcome in such a readable narrative that it's almost as if I were right there with her every step of the way."

Margaret "Sam" Sansom,
Author of *George the Alligator Finds a Home*

"Lori is a strong, kind, generous soul, committed to doing good in the world. Her story is a triumph of will, perseverance, and determination. If you are looking for an example of how to NOT take NO for an answer, this is the book for you!"

Cheryl Herrick, Founder, Ponytail Racing
and Racing for Warriors

To Mike...
for helping me to find "Lori"

ACKNOWLEDGMENTS

With loving gratitude to my Heavenly Father who leads and guides me and whose errand I am on. Thank you for helping me to see my divine potential and for placing people along life's path with the gifts and talents to make this book a reality and with the vision to make all that is yet to come possible.

To My Family...

To my husband, Mike, for believing in me and loving me through all the ups and downs of life. For telling me I was beautiful when I could not yet see it. And especially for giving me the latitude to explore and figure out who "Lori" is, even when you could not yet see the necessity for the path I had chosen to take. Your encouragement, support, and safe space to heal old wounds has allowed me to blossom, grow, and become the woman Heavenly Father intended me to be and accomplish all that I am here to do. You are my BFF and eternal companion. Ours is a forever love!

To my boys, Christopher and Joshua, who have honed my parenting skills with your own tenacity and resolve. I am so proud of the men and fathers you have become. Thank you for being the inspiration that keeps me ever moving forward and wanting to be a better parent and person. "I love you more!"

To my parents for teaching me how to work hard and never give up. For loving me in spite of, or maybe because of, my strong will. I know you send up many prayers on my behalf. I am stronger for having been your daughter. I love you both and hope I have made you proud.

To my sister, Tammy, for your love and support and for our friendship that is forever growing stronger.

To my eight magnificent grandchildren Marlie, Shayleigh, Aaden, Aubrie, Chayton, Adeline, Rowan, and Aedan—I am so grateful for every moment we get to spend together. You are amazing and Mima loves you! Always remember, "Life is about choices," and "You are stronger than you think you are!"

To All of My Past and Present Teachers, Mentors, and Coaches...

To Mr. (Norman) Klump, you were the first person willing to take a chance on me and whose sign over our junior high band room door—"There is no stupid question, if asked sincerely."—empowered me to seek answers to life's difficult questions when I felt so small and insignificant.

To Mrs. (Ann) Dassow, my high school business law teacher, you taught me to choose my first instinct and that I would be correct a majority of the time. You made such a difference during those rough teenage years. Thank you for believing in me.

To Coach Jack Cheyne, you were not only one of my favorite teachers (psychology), but made me feel that I mattered when you took the time to listen to that sixteen-year-old girl, as you shared with me the fine art of sports taping and wrapping. Thank you for your selfless service, love, and counsel.

To Phil, my life-coach and mentor, you are always willing to "call it like you see it" and have helped me to recognize that I can be anything I dare dream to be. Thank you for believing in me and this book, and for introducing me to Amanda. You forever changed my life's trajectory.

To Brandon, your chiropractic skills are just one of the gifts you've brought to my life. Thank you for being a friend, confidante, team player, and for being "in tune" to be the vehicle God used to kick my butt in gear and show me this book was not for posterity's sake but for all those whom He can heal through my story.

To Margaret (Sam) Sansom, for your selfless love and devotion to my growth and transformation, as well as checking in at just the right moment to see where I was in writing my book—and for never allowing room for any excuses. I will be forever grateful. Thank you for being able to see the vision and how it could change the lives of many. I am so grateful our paths and hearts have not only intersected but are intertwined.

To LeeAnn Pulliam, for "seeing" me and believing in me, in so many ways, before I ever believed in myself and for not only encouraging me to run that first race, but supporting me at nearly every race along the way!

To My Team...

To Amanda, my writing coach, mentor, and ally. You continually amaze me with your superpowers and intuitive intellect, knowing just the right verbiage needed to make a point and/or create a major shift in momentum. Together we have laughed and cried through the process of healing old wounds, always astonished at how similar our childhood experiences were. Your gifts are many, and I am so much better for having known and worked with you. Your love and support continue to help me grow and become all that Heavenly Father wants me to be. Thank you most of all for empowering me to see that I have inside me the innate ability to script my own story, to dream my own dreams, and to make those dreams my reality! Oh... and let's not forget a huge shout-out for the challenge to write that dang vulnerability contract, which was just what I needed to launch me forward, giving me the clarity and momentum to rewrite the generational stories holding me hostage, fulfill my childhood dream of writing a children's book, strengthen my marriage, and so much more!

To Alyssa Noelle Coelho, you are one of the most gifted creatives I've ever encountered, and that I get to call you my friend is an extra special bonus! Thank you for sharing your special talents to create this magnificent cover that magically draws people to pick it up and look inside. You're the best!

To Dianne, for reading, editing, and teaching me so much more than all of my English teachers and professors combined. For your friendship, patience, support, and belief in me throughout this healing and writing journey. I love you, my friend.

To Dawn Teagarden, for the fabulous job you did on the interior design of the book. It is beautiful.

To Brylee Allred, for creating the signpost logo and other illustrations throughout the book. You are creative beyond your sixteen years, and I can't wait for everyone to see your work in the Cousin Camp Chronicles series.

To My Community...

To my fellow messengers and allies, who gave me a safe place to share, learn, and transform. Thank you for all your incredible ideas, encouraging words, and networks you shared with me along the way.

To all of the readers who previewed this book, thank you for making time to read and provide the priceless feedback you shared and for your encouraging words along the way. This book is even better because of you!

With the Upmost Love and Gratitude,

CONTENTS

Prologue

THE ACCIDENT

Backing up into our graveled circle drive, I pointed the Expedition toward the street. As was my usual custom, I paused for a moment to mentally "check in" before deciding which way to turn. Either direction would lead me to Joshua's school. Really, the only difference was a change of scenery.

I began to turn left toward the center of town and then glanced at the clock.

Hmmm. Just enough time to make the copies and mail this package of scrapbook pages before I pick Joshua up from school. I'd love to check one more item off my huge list of things to do!

I turned right out of the driveway toward the print shop and was deep in thought while traversing the five-mile trip to town.

Christmas is quickly approaching and still so much to accomplish!

Momentarily grabbing my attention was the beauty of the Rocky Mountains, looming majestically in the distance with their snow-topped peaks.

I love this view! Keep the snow there, I mused.

Then I glanced across the open fields, noticing the winter wheat was already poking its head up out of the ground.

Turning right at the country road, I followed the far west end of the wheat field across the rolling hills toward the edge of town.

As I started up the first hill, a clear and distinct voice said, *"You need to slow down."* I had heard this voice speak this loudly only once before, as I was asking for heavenly guidance about which church to join.

I looked at the speedometer. *Hmm...* I was going 50 in a 45-mph zone. *Five over isn't that fast, but...* I sighed audibly, knowing this might affect my timing. *The last time the voice spoke to me and I followed its guidance, it changed my life forever. I'll slow down.*

I tapped the brake gently, lowering my speed to the posted 45 mph limit as I reached midway up the incline. Seconds later, cresting the hill, I noticed a garbage truck pulling out of a subdivision to my left; and nearly a mile in front of me was a semi-truck with a big candy cane tied to the front, toward the bottom of the second hill.

How festive. I smiled to myself.

We were the only three vehicles traversing this paved country road—or so I thought.

A split-second later, bursting onto the scene directly in front of me was a small, white sedan, coming at me, in MY LANE...

HOLY CRAP!

The instant it materialized, I found myself peering directly into the windshield of the oncoming car. The driver was so close that I could clearly see the expression of sheer panic on her face, her eyes wide open in terror.

Instantly, that same clear and distinct voice that I had heard moments earlier, now urgently warned me, *"You CANNOT hit this lady!"*

Where did she even come from? It was like she had appeared out of thin air, jetting back from a time portal that dropped her directly in front of me. I scanned the road, instinctively taking in my options in the few moments I had before we would collide.

I cranked my steering wheel sharply to the right to avoid impact. She whizzed by and went into a spin. I swung my head around to see where her car was heading before looking back out my windshield, where I quickly realized my truck had traversed 10 to 15 feet, left the pavement, and was headed into the bar ditch.

The next thing I saw was a 20-inch cement culvert directly in front of me. With no time to stop, or react, impact was imminent. I quickly jerked the steering wheel back to the left, hitting the culvert square on the right front tire, which blew the tire on impact and launched my Expedition thirty feet forward into the air, passenger side door facing the sky. Scrapbook pages, library books, and my cell phone flew around the cabin.

It was like I was watching this all happen from above. There was no panic or terror—only peace and calm. I had listened to the voice and done all I could do. What happened next was completely out of my control.

Descending hood first and leaning driver's side near the ground, the vehicle touched down, hitting the pavement initially on the left front tire and then on the left back tire, and continued traveling another twenty feet on two wheels before finally tilting back upright, landing all four wheels on the ground.

I came to an abrupt halt as the rim of the blown tire dug deep into the soft shoulder of the road, and I looked down to see the pages, books, and cell phone in a crumpled heap at my feet.

I quickly threw open the door and climbed out of the Expedition, not believing what had just happened. The semi-truck driver had managed to stop his truck on the other side of the road and just to the north of where my wild ride had deposited me.

Fearing the worst, he frantically ran across the road, crying out, "Are you okay? Are you okay?" Out of breath and in complete disbelief of what he had just witnessed, he spewed, "That was some pretty fancy driving! How did you keep from rolling that truck? I can't believe you didn't roll your truck!"

Surprisingly, I still did not feel any panic or terror and, considering what I had just experienced, remained incredibly calm. The words escaped my lips in an almost inaudible whisper, "It wasn't me." Thinking back through the last few moments, I said it again more confidently, "It wasn't ME!" I continued, "I could sense, almost see, Heavenly Father's hands reach down out of heaven and grasp hold of my truck as if it were a Tonka toy. Like a toddler playing cars and trucks, He picked me up on impact and carried me through the air, setting me gently down on the other side."

Just like He had done so many times before...

Introduction

ACCIDENTS OR CHOICES?

After we called the police and loved ones, I went to check on the other driver. Someone was with her, but I wanted to check on her myself. As I mounted the hill to where her car had stopped, I couldn't quite shake the experience of hearing the Spirit's prompting.

I had known from the first moment I had seen her through my windshield that she was an older lady. As I reached her vehicle, the person with her stood up, folded her arms, and stared at me. I noticed her piercing eyes, like daggers ready to cut me to pieces, and lips pursed together in a scowl. She glared protectively, as if somehow, what had transpired was entirely my fault. I introduced myself, and she informed me she was the woman's daughter and that she and her husband had heard the accident from their home in the subdivision just west of the country road, and had come to see what was going on.

It is quite a coincidence to arrive at the scene of an accident so quickly and find that one of the drivers just happens to be her mother, who was wildly driving her car in the wrong lane and was supposedly going past the subdivision entrance.

I shook my head to clear the thought, blowing it off for the time being. Moving past the younger woman, I leaned down to address the elderly lady. She appeared to be in her seventies, with silver hair, dark eyes, and a tired expression.

What's that? I noticed the tube coming out of her nostrils. *Oh my gosh.* My eyes flashed to the daughter and then back inside the car where I discovered she was not wearing her seatbelt.

Leaning over the open window, I calmly asked her, "Did you have your seatbelt on?"

She replied rather timidly, glancing toward the oxygen tank sitting in the bucket seat with her, "No. My oxygen tank gets in the way." It was then that I noticed the canister of oxygen.

How did I overlook that?

My mind started spinning back to the warning that had shot through my head just a few moments before, *"You CANNOT hit this lady!"* I sucked in a breath as if the air had suddenly been knocked out of my lungs.

Overcome with what could have been, I sternly and matter-of-factly asked, "Do you realize—if I had hit you, I could have killed you?!"

The realization of what could have happened sent my body whirling with anger, frustration, and most of all fear. I did the only thing I could at that moment. I turned abruptly in the direction of my vehicle, thoughts swirling and spiraling in my head. It was obvious to me that she was not injured, and I knew I had to leave before I said anything more.

I stormed back down the hill, trying to regain my composure, and silently thanking my Heavenly Father for allowing our vehicles to narrowly escape collision. I expressed my gratitude for His hand in miraculously keeping us all safe that day. Oh my... the *what if's* that rushed across my mind. I was so grateful I didn't have anyone else in the car with me.

"Thank you, Lord," was all I could say.

As I continued my descent down the hill, I kept seeing her face through my windshield, hearing the voice going through my head, and thinking, *What if I had not swerved when I did?* I could see in my mind, the Expedition climbing right over the top of her little car and exploding, blowing us both to kingdom come. A shiver went through me as I again saw the image of her terrified face looking back at me through the windshield as my vehicle came barreling toward her. This scene was forever etched in my mind.

The two truck drivers were deep in conversation next to my truck. As I approached, they completed their conversation and asked me if the other driver was okay and who was with her. I answered their questions and told them about the seatbelt, the oxygen tank, and how I had heard a voice warning me not to hit her seconds before impact.

We were all just standing there in silent disbelief. A truck flying through the air, rolling down the road on two wheels, oxygen tanks, seatbelts, heavenly voices... It was a lot to take in!

Where are those police? Why aren't they here yet? I impatiently wondered to myself before sarcastically commenting, "It's a good thing no one was injured!"

Again, my thoughts returned to the image of my truck climbing over the top of her car and both vehicles exploding into flames.

STOP IT! I brazenly lectured myself. *That is not what happened! You listened. You slowed down. Oh, thank the*

Lord that you slowed down! And, most importantly, that you did not hit her. Lori, you did as you were guided and everyone was blessed accordingly.

In the distance, I could hear the sirens.

Finally, I thought. I just wanted this to all be over so I could go home. Two police cars drove into view. A female officer stepped out of the first vehicle, walked toward our group of three, and inquired as to injuries.

"As far as I know, no one has been seriously injured. The vehicles did not actually collide, but my Expedition hit the culvert and—"

I was about to finish my brief explanation when she asked me to wait.

The next forty-five minutes or so were filled with completing tons of paperwork, answering questions, waiting, and then answering more questions. It seemed like we would never be finished. As I stood with my husband, Mike, who had arrived shortly after the police, waiting for the okay to leave, I started feeling a shooting pain go down my right leg.

What in the world? I winced and Mike wanted to know what had happened. We were just standing there. I saw the look of concern in his kind, brown eyes. Realizing the shock must be wearing off because my body was starting to ache all over, I approached the policewoman and explained the aching pain and the sudden sharp pains going down the back of my leg. I asked her to please make a note of it in her report.

Dutifully, she asked, "Do you want me to call for an ambulance?"

I'm sure that is standard procedure.

Oh yeah... That's all I need, I thought to myself. All we needed was one more bill to pay. Ambulance, hospital bills, I was seeing dollar signs form before my very eyes.

"No, thank you," I replied. "I will make an appointment with our family physician when I get home." She asked me a second time and, again, I declined the offer. Shortly thereafter, the police officer finally gave me permission to leave.

By the time Mike and I arrived home, Joshua and Chris were both there. Inquiring minds wanted to know, so I sat down in my desk chair and set about telling all three of them exactly what had transpired.

In my attempt to explain, I became more and more irritated. As I rehearsed the details, something was different. This time, I suddenly remembered that when the truck landed on the left front tire and then the left back, I had literally been hanging from my seat belt. I could see the books flying at me, pelting me. Then, I recalled seeing black with white flecks screaming past me.

What the heck? What was it that was black?

"Did you hit your head?" Mike anxiously inquired, his eyes wide with concern.

Chris, already nineteen, chimed in with adult-like concern, "Did you black out?"

I knew that I had not hit my head or blacked out. No, this was definitely very different. I was becoming increasingly frustrated. No matter how hard I tried, I simply could not remember.

Blast it! Everything had happened so fast.

Sitting by, unusually quiet, watching and taking it all in, Joshua's nearly twelve-year-old body looked smaller than normal. He sat in a crumpled bundle on the floor, his arms wrapped around his knees. Looking back and forth between the three of us as the conversation escalated, a mixture of fear and confusion crossed his face. Mike and Chris were hurling questions at me, which only agitated me further. I felt the walls closing in around me and instinctively stood up, as if to push the walls back into place. I did not know the answers.

How could I not know? Why can I not remember? I played it over and over in my mind. I wanted to scream, *I DON'T KNOW!*

Then, as if I had been struck suddenly by a bolt of lightning or smacked on the head with a 2x4, it hit me. I knew what it was! As I had literally been hanging, suspended by my seat belt, traveling precariously on two wheels, I had automatically, due to gravity, been forced to look out my side window at the pavement zinging by. The black with specks was the street.

Wow! I burst into tears, all the pent-up emotions exploding. The realization of all that had just happened hit me like a ton of bricks. I collapsed in a heap in the chair, sobbing uncontrollably.

I could have so easily rolled the truck, flipped several times, and slammed into the semi-truck driver. Oh my goodness! Sobs emanated from deep within my soul. I had definitely been protected by my Heavenly Father.

It was almost as if Father in Heaven had said, "No, my little one. You still have much more work to complete here. You must stay a while longer."

The boys stared at me, not knowing exactly what to do. They had never seen this emotional side of their mother before, nor had Mike. Not to this degree. I could not force myself to think about them as wave after wave of sobs erupted, shaking and convulsing my body.

I finally managed to get control of my emotions, for the moment, when I noticed that I was growing achier by the minute. I winced again and grabbed the arm of my chair. The pain in my buttocks and leg was shooting through me as if someone were stabbing me with an ice pick. I knew I had to call the doctor's office and get in immediately. Something was not right.

I contacted the doctor's office and scheduled an appointment within the hour, but Mike had to get back to the office to finish his paperwork and meet each of the construction crews as they came in for the evening. I could tell he was struggling with having to leave me, not really knowing what was wrong. Chris volunteered to take me to the doctor. We decided this was the best option since I no longer had a vehicle or a desire to get back in a car at all, let alone drive.

I assured Mike that I would call him as soon as I knew anything. I had no idea what tests they might run, what x-rays would be taken, or how long it would be before we would get any results.

He gave me a kiss and a hug, and I nearly burst into tears again. I managed to contain the tears until after he left.

I don't want him worrying any more than he already is. It was unlike me to be so upset and cry. I am usually a pretty tough cookie. But right then. Well, I was feeling more like a marshmallow. *What is happening to me? Where did that tough girl go? Come back!! PLEASE!*

My life changed forever that day.

I woke up at 3 a.m. to help my son with his paper route, prepped for the day, took him to seminary and then school, kissed my husband as he left for work, and blew through a million little to-do's at home before getting in the car that morning. I had no idea that it was the last time, for a long time, that I would be capable of a daily routine like that.

Because of the injuries I sustained in the accident, it took me more than twelve years to recover—physically, mentally, and emotionally—but I did it. And every day, the message that was confirmed to me over and over was, "Life is about choices." I could choose to stay committed to believing, hoping, and working for my full recovery; or I could choose to give up and give into the pain, take the meds the doctors were pushing on me, and settle into anger, resentment, bitterness, and fear about everything I had lost in just a few minutes on a back country road.

In a split second, I went from being a physically active, energetic, productive "do-it-myself" wife, mother of two children, and leader at the church to wondering how I was going to get up/down the basement stairs to work, find the energy to prepare dinner, and eventually gather the strength to step into the shower or roll over in bed on my own.

Normal, everyday tasks I had previously taken for granted became something to strive toward... being able to... possibly do again... someday. But that wasn't the end of my story.

Remember, I knew from the very beginning that I had been protected by my Heavenly Father, so part of my work, beyond the physical recovery, was figuring out *why* He had saved me. And THAT journey—well, that's the one that really surprised me.

What I learned about myself and God, and what we have accomplished together—building a community, running half marathons and other endurance and long-distance races, owning my own company, traveling, and continuing my activities with the youth at church—are nothing short of a bunch of tiny little miracles.

I have learned that there are no accidents. There are only choices.

If you have picked up this book, chances are that you are also facing some sort of trial. Maybe it's the fallout from an accident or injury, maybe it's an abusive relationship that you are trying to free yourself from, or maybe it is some tragedy that happened to you as a child.

Whatever the situation, my hope for you as you read this book is that you will find the courage and determination to reach deep inside yourself, find your resolve, and make the choice to keep moving forward and find the healing for your individual situation.

Your circumstances and details are undoubtedly very different from mine, and you may witness my recovery and wonder if something like it is possible for you. Truth be told, if you have suffered a worse accident or injury, you may not be able to do exactly what I have been able to do, but that does not mean you are not capable of far more. And I pray this story will inspire you to reach for more of what is possible for you. To support you as you navigate your own journey—through the slowing down, the swerving around obstacles, the pain, the triage, and especially the momentum that can unfold in your life once you have the tools for growth and healing—I have included short reflections and prompts at the end of each chapter. If you have a journal, I'd recommend you write out your thoughts and feelings as you go, as it will speed up your own healing process.

My prayer is that in my story, you will see the lessons you are ready for, recognize where you can apply them to your situation, and give yourself permission to heal and move into the space that I believe Heavenly Father is holding just for you—a space where you can see all the ways that His grace has carried you and saved your life so you can do the work you are here to do. A space where you, too, come to realize that there are no accidents. There are only choices.

"Slowing down is sometimes the best way to speed up."

Mike Vance

Visionary, Strategist, Speaker

Choice #1

Chris opened the car door, and I slid cautiously into the passenger seat of his silver, two-door Saturn. Making sure I was completely inside the vehicle, he closed the door.

"You okay?" he asked tentatively, climbing in behind the wheel and starting the car.

"Besides feeling like I'm sitting on the ground," I half-heartedly teased, "I'm fine."

He gave me one of those teenaged-boy looks, rolling his blue eyes like, *Yeah right, Mom,* and started driving to the doctor's office, glancing my way every few seconds to confirm I was still okay. I must not have been hiding my experience well. I was feeling every little bump in the road, and by the time we reached our destination, I was hurting from head to toe.

I'm glad I decided not to take any over-the-counter pain medication. I don't want to mask any symptoms. But OUCH!

We pulled into the entrance of the medical center and found a place to park, and I waited for Chris to open my door.

So, this is what it feels like to be an old lady, I thought as he grasped hold of my elbow, lifting me slowly and gently out of the car. *And just yesterday, I was romping and playing with the kids.*

As we walked through the front door, stark white walls and the smell of antiseptic overwhelmed my senses. It took only a few minutes to check in and fill out the second batch of paperwork for the day. Not long after we returned the papers to the receptionist, they called my name. I patted Chris's hand and headed back on my own.

There are just some things a son shouldn't have to do at nineteen.

I followed the seasoned nurse through the door and past the hustle and bustle of a baby crying as his naked body was placed on a cold scale to be weighed, and I noticed other nurses who were busily shuffling patients here and there. My nurse stopped outside a door at the end of the hall and, with a sullen expression, routinely motioned me to go in. I sat down on the table and she proceeded to take my blood pressure and temperature.

"All normal." Her voice was monotone and void of emotion as she roughly removed the cuff from my arm.

"I'm not surprised. My blood pressure normally runs on the low side," I responded, in an attempt to make her aware that it might be higher than normal.

"The doctor will be with you shortly," she said curtly, without even responding or acknowledging my comment. She grabbed the file and closed the door, leaving me in the cold, sterile silence.

I wanted to shout after her, "Thanks for listening," but I decided to keep my thoughts and growing upset to myself.

Maybe I am just being sensitive. Looking away from the door, I glanced around the room. On the counter to my right stood glass jars filled with cotton balls, swabs, and tongue depressors all neatly stacked in a row. There was a stainless-steel sink with hand sanitizer. Magazines hung from a plastic tray on the opposite wall, placed strategically next to a chair.

With no windows to look out and nothing but the aching in my body to occupy me, my mind quickly became bored with the décor and wandered back to the accident, playing it over again in my mind. *"Slow down! You cannot hit this woman."* The swerve. The papers flying around me. The black flecks just outside my window.

Suddenly, the door popped open, startling me back to the present. In marched the slender female doctor, sporting a short bob hair cut that swayed as she walked. She had on a dark pant suit and white lab coat from which she pulled a pen from the pocket as she asked flippantly, "So what seems to be our problem today?"

"I was in a car accident earlier today," I timidly began. Over the next ten minutes, she listened dutifully to my story and appeared to have jotted down some quick notes. Then she started her examination.

"Lie on your stomach," she ordered.

I slowly rolled over onto my stomach and she commenced with the twisting, bending, poking and prodding.

"Does this hurt?" she asked.

Define hurt, I thought. With my high threshold for pain, I wasn't sure how to respond. I did not want to make it more than it was, but I also did not want to make it less than either. "A little," I finally answered, unsure of how to describe what I was experiencing. How do you determine what level of pain you are feeling and correctly describe it to someone who has likely never experienced this type of pain before?

She let out a deep sigh, as if annoyed, and snapped, "On a scale from 1-10, with 1 being no pain and 10 being excruciating, what is it?"

Again, this depends on your perspective, I reasoned to myself before answering, "About a three or maybe a four, but I have a pretty high pain tolerance."

No response.

Did you hear me? I wanted to say out loud.

She continued her exam, and I answered with a varying degree of low numbers until she did something that made me almost yelp, "Nine! That was a *nine!*"

"Stand up and walk across the room for me," she said sternly, with no sign of compassion or concern for any pain I might have experienced in her voice.

I slowly unrolled myself from the fetal position and, climbing gingerly off the table, began walking across the room.

"Now bend over and touch your toes," she barked harshly as I reached the wall.

I turned around and obediently bent over and touched my toes... almost.

That's strange, I thought. *Normally, I am pretty flexible. Touching my toes is no big deal.*

As I straightened back up, a pain shot down the back of my leg and into my heel and out through my toes, nearly doubling me back over in pain.

I glanced up to see the doctor's reaction, only to find her writing notes in the file and not looking at me at all.

Did she even see what just happened?

"That was another *nine*," I emphasized, hoping to elicit some kind of response.

"Go ahead and sit back down on the table. I'll be right back. I just need to grab my prescription pad."

Not exactly the feedback I was looking for.

After what seemed to be an exorbitant amount of time, she finally found her way back into the room. Handing me two prescriptions, she said, "Take these. One is an anti-depressant and the other is a pain killer."

I took the two prescriptions and responded matter-of-factly, wanting her to understand that I would choose what I believed was best for me, "I won't be filling either of these. I don't do anti-depressants and I don't do pain killers."

Looking at me, mouth open in disbelief, she replied with even more condescension, "Maybe you just don't understand."

Understand what? You haven't told me anything! I was about to verbalize this thought when she launched into her explanation.

"What you need to come to grips with is that you have PTSD. Do you even know what that is?"

"Yes. It's what many of our brave soldiers who have been in combat come home with," I replied dryly, not knowing where she was going and not appreciating her demeaning attitude.

"Correct. Although, anyone who has experienced a traumatic event can have PTSD, not just soldiers."

Somehow this did not set well with me. Combat soldiers go through so much and to state that just anyone can have PTSD, not to mention the prescribed "treatment," seemed to take something away from all those who serve our country so bravely.

"I only had a car accident. I was not fighting a war," I countered. "Are there no other options before we go jumping into psych medications and pain pills?"

"Doesn't matter," she snapped unrelentingly, while simultaneiously locking her hands on her hips and glowering, as if daring me to defy her "professional" diagnosis, and ignoring my question.

Sure, it doesn't matter to you, I muttered in my head. *Just get her hooked on psych drugs and pain pills so we can keep her mind focused on everything she can't do, wallowing in self-pity and immobilized by fear, while forcing her to continue coming back to us for more. Let's not find a solution.* Oh, how I disliked doctors!

"But I am in pain," I tried again. "What is causing me to hurt so badly when I move just so?"

"That's what the pain killers are for," she responded as though she only heard half of the question.

Taking a deep breath, I persisted once last time. "Isn't there an x-ray, MRI, or physical therapy that I should be considering? Something that will help me heal, not just mask the pain?"

Glaring at me, she said, "I will prescribe twenty physical therapy visits for you, but I don't think they will help. What you need are the anti-depressants and pain killers." She scribbled on her pad, violently ripped off the page, and tossed the physical therapy script in my direction.

I had definitely stepped on her toes, but she stepped on mine first. Between the pain and the doctor not listening to anything I said, I was not a happy camper and in no mood for her attitude.

"I want to see you back in a couple of weeks. And take the meds," she shot back with exasperation in her tone as she zipped out the door, slamming it behind her.

I hate it when they don't listen.

She had no idea, but this was not my first rodeo with doctors like her. There was one that had taught me the importance of second opinions and making the choice to listen to my gut.

I was three months pregnant when my first husband and I were married, and I turned nineteen just six weeks before Christopher was born on a military base in California—a long way from where I had grown up in Colorado and anyone that I really knew.

I was two weeks past my due date and the decision was made to induce labor. When the back labor started, they gave me a spinal block. The contractions were just a few minutes apart when Christopher's heart rate suddenly dropped from 140 down to 60, then 50, then 45. Doctors and nurses went into hyperdrive, flitting around the room.

One attendant asked my husband to go out in the hall with him, where he signed papers regarding who should live if the choice needed to be made. Then, they urgently wheeled me into the delivery room where they proceeded to use forceps to deliver Christopher as quickly as possible.

A couple of weeks later, I took Christopher to his first "well baby" appointment. The Naval doctor began his examination, and Christopher immediately fussed at being handled. The doctor poked and prodded while I questioned why he would not turn his head and would only nurse contentedly on one side. When I would attempt to nurse on the other breast, he would scream and cry in pain.

Handing my son back to me, the doctor nonchalantly informed me, "It is just a hematoma... a bruise."

Then he gave me an exercise to do with him. I was to set Christopher between my legs, holding him in an upright position, and use my hands to turn his neck gently this way and that several times each day.

"It will eventually work itself out," the doctor informed me.

I had not had a lot of experience with doctors, and I had no reason to doubt that they knew what they were doing. They had gone to school, graduated, and, by putting them on a pedestal, I somehow felt that they were a step above me for having received their degree.

Never once did I think that maybe I would know more about a situation than they did; but that all changed three months later when I went home to Colorado with Christopher shortly after Christmas.

My parents were anxious to see us, and my husband was going to be out in the field for a couple of weeks. While visiting, I decided to see my chiropractor and ask him about Christopher and the diagnosis. He took one look at Christopher and told me to get him to a chiropractor he knew, whose specialty was working with children, as quickly as possible.

On the very first visit, the doctor began a special procedure with Christopher called skull molding. We were able to see him a couple of times before I received the phone call that would send my life spiraling off in yet another direction and delay further treatment for Christopher. The Marine Corp chaplain on the other end of the line explained that my husband had been out on a military exercise and had double-fed a mortar and lost his right hand just above his wrist. He was in a hospital in Palm Springs, and I was to come home immediately.

After five months of hospitals, surgery, and fighting with the military, we moved back to Colorado to be near family as he recuperated, and the military figured out what to do with him, as they no longer considered him "fit for duty" as a grunt in the Marine Corp.

Upon our return to Colorado, I took Christopher to the chiropractor again, and the skull molding continued until one day just a few days before his third birthday. It wasn't until that appointment that the doctor explained the full consequences of his quick actions.

"Remember when you first brought Christopher to me and I felt inside his mouth and worked on his skull?" he questioned kindly, compassion emanating from his bright blue eyes.

"Oh yes," I said as I nodded my head, affirming that memory.

How could I forget that?

"Well, the roof of your mouth, is the bottom of your brain," he began. "When I felt the roof of Chris's mouth that first day, it was completely deformed. When this happens, we usually have about three years to make corrections before the soft spot in the baby's skull is solid and can no longer be manipulated. Today Chris is a normal, healthy boy. Had you not come to me when you did, he would be permanently deformed and mentally retarded."

I'm sure my jaw dropped to the floor. This information was completely new to me. I was so grateful for this chiropractor and his expertise and the care he had given my precious son, and so angry at the military doctor for brushing him off with a few stupid and useless exercises.

Yeah, I am not going to be brushed off by this doctor. Something isn't right in my body, and I'm going to get to the bottom of it before I have slowed to a complete stop.

Collecting my jacket and purse, my thoughts turned to my grown son who was still in the waiting room, anticipating my return. As I walked back toward him, I thought about his life.

He loved playing soccer and he took it seriously, playing in travel tournament teams since he was eleven and on the varsity squad as a sophomore in high school, and eventually making the second-string state team his senior year. He was an avid reader and had graduated near the top of his class, having taken every math and science class the high school offered, including calculus and trigonometry.

Yet all of this could have been so drastically different had I not been prompted to ask another doctor's opinion. It was no accident. By choosing to act on this simple prompting, Christopher's life, and mine, were changed forever.

Walking out of the room and toward the receptionist, my mind was swirling with frustration.

Why did I even bother? Maybe I should have taken the ambulance ride that was offered.

After scheduling my next appointment, I motioned to Chris that I was ready to leave.

As we walked to the car, Chris asked, "How did it go, Mom?"

I just shook my head, "Let's wait until we get to the car and I'll call Dad. That way, you can both hear the diagnosis at the same time." I didn't think I had the strength in me to go over it more than once.

Seated in the car, I dialed Mike's phone, put it on speaker, and gave them the details of my appointment.

"She didn't even want to take an x-ray?" Mike asked in disbelief.

"Nope! I felt like the only thing she wanted me to do was to take the anti-depressants, and I am *not* going to do that!"

"Did she at least say what might have caused the shooting pains?" Mike prodded, his voice overflowing with concern.

"*No,*" I responded curtly. "The only things she said was that I had PTSD and that I was to take the anti-depressants and the pain killers." Overcome with pain, I paused the conversation, "Mike, we are almost home and I am going to lie down for a while."

Before I laid down, I managed to call the two physical therapists the doctor had recommended, and scheduled an appointment with one of them for the following week. As soon as I curled up on the couch to rest, I fell into a deep sleep. It was peaceful until the end, when I saw the woman's face again. Only this time, there was no warning voice as her car came toward me. I hit her head on, driving up and over the top of her, the two cars exploding into flames.

I sat bolt upright on the couch, completely out of breath. The room was dark, and I must have cried out because Mike came rushing in from the kitchen.

Sitting down next to me and holding me like a child, he attempted to comfort me, "It's okay, Sweetie. You were just having a dream." He rocked me back and forth in an attempt to calm my sobbing, not knowing how many times he would do this again after the many nightmares that would follow in the coming months.

The next week was full of anticipation that the doctor would figure out what was wrong and chart the way to healing my body. Unfortunately, nothing was resolved at that initial doctor's appointment or any subsequent visits to the doctor.

I switched to my family doctor after not getting anywhere again with his colleague during our second appointment. I informed him of his partner's insistence on my taking the meds, but he shrugged it off as if it were no big deal and nonchalantly asked, "Do you still have enough physical therapy visits?"

I really must be invisible, I surmised. *If Mike were here, I wouldn't be treated this way.*

"Yes," I said, responding to his question. "She also suggested it might be beneficial for me to see a massage therapist weekly."

"We can accommodate that," he said, whipping out his script pad and scribbling another prescription. As he handed me the paper, he said, "You really should think about taking the meds." And then he was out the door.

Over the next several months, my health continued to decline. The pain became so intense that my body would randomly decide it was done and shut down, causing me to fall asleep. My grip also seemed to have a mind of its own, as one minute I would be holding a glass, and the next minute it would shatter on the ground, sending its contents flying in all directions.

By the end of April, the physical therapist was beside herself that I was not improving and suggested I ask for a TENS unit. I, too, was growing weary of all the appointments and additional stretches and exercises, and still no sign of improvement. This was not the way this was supposed to go. I was doing everything I could to improve, and it seemed I was being knocked backwards every time I tried to make progress. I determined to get my courage up and ask if there was something we could do about the fatigue at my next visit.

Being courageous is something I've had to be my entire life, I thought, drifting back to one of my earliest memories.

I was around five years old, listening to my mom and dad fighting from the next room. Dad sounded really angry. This fight was going nowhere good, and I stealthily walked toward the commotion to make sure mom was okay. We barely had money to pay our rent and put food on the table, as my parents had finally closed the candy store that, with the rising cost of butter and sugar, was creating a smaller and smaller profit margin on which to live.

On this particular day, Mom had questioned his need for the tape recorder he had purchased. This was the wrong thing to do. The conversation escalated and then took a turn for the worse when Dad reached out to grab her.

This was not going to go well, my young mind calculated; and fearing what Dad would do to Mom, I resolutely ran from the corner and sprang onto Dad's back in an attempt to stop him, knocking his glasses off his face. They went flying up into the air, then skipped across the floor, and fell to the ground on the other side of the tiny kitchen. This promptly redirected his anger toward me.

After a painful whooping for getting involved in something that was "none of my business," I walked through the doorway to where my mom was sitting on one of the beds in the small room my sister and I shared. Mom was comforting my younger sister who had been crying and turned to me as I walked into the room, head hanging in defeat. Shuffling up next to her, I looked up as she said, almost in a whisper, "If you would just keep your mouth shut..."

"But, Mom," I boldly interrupted. "He shouldn't hit," I countered with my five-year-old logic.

Speaking sternly, she continued, "If you'd just kept your mouth shut, Lori—just shut up—none of this would have happened to you."

In my mind, Mom needed to be protected. She did not fight back because being quiet and just accepting the consequences of stepping out of line was what she did to make the argument come to an end. To me, it was just wrong and I could not—NO, I *would* not—choose to just sit back and be quiet. Not at five years old—not ever.

At my next appointment, I asked if there were something else we could do to figure out the cause of the fatigue. He drew multiple vials of blood and sent them to the lab where they ran a Chem 12 panel and a thyroid test. When he reminded me that the meds were really all I needed to improve my situation, I felt my face get hot and my blood pressure skyrocket. The veins in my neck and forehead popped out from the increased pressure. Something had better change soon or I was going to blow.

My schedule was filled with physical and massage therapy treatments as well as regular bimonthly visits to the doctor. I also continued the tasks of teaching my scrapbooking workshops, working with the young women at church, collecting and filling orders for my wholesale foods business, and homeschooling Joshua for half of his sixth-grade classes. Every one of these tasks was becoming increasingly difficult to accomplish, and I was tired of how slow my participation in life had become.

In May, when the bloodwork came back negative, I convinced the doctor to do a back x-ray. When this failed to reveal the cause of my pain, fatigue, and ever-decreasing ability to function, I was so discouraged. By this point, it felt that everyone, even Mike, was doubting that I was truly injured. I didn't have any physical evidence of injury, like a broken arm or a massive gash on my face.

Maybe it IS all in my head, I thought as I tossed and turned in bed late one night, trying to make sense of it all. My mind flashed back to another time, long before, when someone tried to convince me that something was all in my head.

It was winter time, and I was all bundled up in coat, hat, and gloves in the back seat of Mom and Dad's drab olive, early 1970s station wagon, sporting faux wood panels on the outside. We were headed for church, and Dad had the heater cranked up. Warm air was enveloping me and I was so hot that I felt like I could throw up. Taking off my gloves, I quietly grabbed hold of the handle and cranked it ever so slightly, creating a small crack between the window and the seal. I leaned against the window so I could feel the coolness of the glass on my face as I sucked the fresh air deep into my lungs.

It was only a moment before Dad yelled, "Lori, close that window!"

"But I'm hot, Dad!" I begged.

"I said, CLOSE that window!" he barked.

"I feel like I am going to throw up," I pleaded, as another wave of nausea swept over me.

"You are not. It's all in your head! Now don't let me catch you rolling that window down again!" His glare in the rear view mirror was so intense, I could feel his anger shoot right through my little body.

It's not in my head, I said to myself. *One of these days I am going to throw up all over you and then you'll see it is not in my head! Then maybe you will listen to me!*

But I never did. The fear of what would happen to me if I threw up in the car was enough to keep it just below heaving threshold.

In the darkness of the night, my common sense quickly brought me back to the present and affirmed me, *No way! The pain I am feeling is real. Maybe they should have to spend a day in this body. Then they would know how incredibly real it is! Do they think I want to feel this way? I didn't ask for any of this!"*

I brought that determination with me through all of the routine appointments and the daily tasks that were becoming more difficult with each passing week. It was near the end of June and we would soon be in Branson, Missouri, for our annual vacation with family and friends. After setting my next appointment for the week after we returned, I walked out into the beautiful, warm sunshine.

What a wonderful change from the doctor's office. I hate how cold those places feel in temperature and support.

The heat felt so good on my face. Summer was my favorite time of the year, and I wanted to spend it reaping the benefits of my garden, playing outside with the kids, and waterskiing.

Will I ever be able to do any of that again? I wondered as I blinked against the sunlight.

I began reminiscing about previous Branson trips. We always had so much fun. Waterskiing on Table Rock Lake, pulling the boys and their friends on tubes, spending a day at Silver Dollar City, with each family taking a turn cooking yummy dinners in the evening at the cabin on the lake. We would all gather together, and everyone would eat their fill before we broke out the card games and desserts, laughing and having a grand time until late into the night.

Oh, what fun we had! I was so eager to experience this time away!

Maybe soaking in the lake and basking in the sun will give me a new perspective, I secretly wished.

Within the week, all the fun activities of previous Branson excursions were back in full swing. After being on the boat for several days and watching everyone else waterski and tube, I made a decision.

If there is nothing wrong with me and it is all in my head, what would it hurt to take a ride around the lake on the skis?

Quickly fastening my life vest and confirming that I wanted to ski, I jumped into the warm Missouri water and strapped on my favorite pair of water skis. Mike circled around and one of the kids tossed me the rope. I grabbed hold and as the rope tightened, I gave the signal for Mike to "hit it." I immediately popped up out of the water, just as I usually did.

Yeah! So far, so good, I thought as I skied for several hundred yards.

Then, it hit me like a huge, crashing wave. This was not a wave of water though, it was a wave of nausea. I immediately made the signal that I was finished and let go of the rope,

Oh no! This can't be happening! What is wrong with me? I can't do anything I enjoy anymore? Am I going to be stuck being a slow, frustrated slug forever?

By the time Mike circled the boat around, I was dizzy and not sure if I was going to make it back onto the craft. As they assisted my climb up the ladder and into the boat, the expression on Mike's face said it all.

"Take me back to the cabin... *now,*" I demanded, barely able to talk. I had turned a ghostly white and was sure I was going to lose my lunch.

Mike docked the boat and helped me into the cabin. He prayed with me before I shooed him off, telling him to go have fun. I just needed to rest. At least, I hoped that was all I required. After several trips to the bathroom, producing nothing but dry heaves, I was finally able to calm my stomach and fell into a deep sleep.

It was so deep that I never heard anyone arrive back at the cabin or make dinner. Mike had tried several times to wake me, to no avail. Beginning to panic, he rustled my shoulders roughly.

"Dinner's ready," he coaxed.

I could hear his voice, but it sounded muffled and far away.

"Come on, George," he tried again, using the nickname he had given me when we were first dating.

This time, I struggled to open my eyes. The room was dark, but I could see the light coming through the doorway from the kitchen and living room. I quickly shut them again to keep out the light. My pounding head felt like it was going to split wide open.

After several more attempts, I eventually woke up and joined everyone for dinner only to return to my bed where I immediately fell back to sleep.

The following morning, I awoke without the headache or nausea.

What was I thinking? I haven't felt like pulling weeds in the garden, let alone water skiing. That was just stupid!

"They told you it was all in your head. What were you supposed to do—sit on the sidelines and watch everyone else having fun?" the other voice in my head countered.

I knew it wasn't in my head! Hmmm... Maybe now someone will believe me.

I did as little as possible over the next couple of days, relaxing in the boat and water, driving the boys on the tubes, and enjoying the trip as much as I could. Yet even during the activities, I kept wondering what I was going to do to figure out the cause of my ailments.

If only Mike would go with me to my appointments...

I sat impatiently on the examining table, waiting for the doctor to make his appearance. I was wondering where we would go from here when he walked in.

"So, how are you doing today?" he asked, the tone in his voice immediately grating on my nerves.

I began my explanation of how I was still in pain and that I would really like to figure out what was going on.

He looked my way and said sharply, "Well, if you would just take the medication—"

That's it! I have endured all I can take. It is time for a "Come to Jesus" meeting!

This was definitely the wrong thing to say to me in that moment. I didn't even let him finish. I glared directly into his dark eyes and leaned toward him so that my face was just inches from his. Then, with all the restraint I could muster to not scream at him, between clenched teeth, I explained the reason for my rage. "I have just come from a ten-day vacation with my family and friends! I am not lying in bed with the covers over my head, not answering my door or my phone. I AM

NOT DEPRESSED—I AM IN PAIN! What are you going to do about it?"

He slowly scooted his wheeled doctor's chair away from the examining table. Pausing only momentarily and then looking up at me, he replied nonchalantly, "I suppose we could do an MRI."

I wanted to tear him limb from limb. *You suppose... You SUPPOSE...* I restated in my mind.

Still glaring at him, I responded curtly, "Well, that would be a nice start!"

He quickly excused himself from the small room and returned momentarily with orders for an MRI. I am sure he thought I was about to go postal. He slid the orders onto the table, telling me to call and make an appointment following the directions he had given me. Then, like a flash, he was gone.

Good riddance! I hope I never have to see you again!

Upon leaving the office, I immediately called Mike and told him what had happened. Feeling proud for advocating for myself, I smirked, "You should have seen the look on his face as he rolled backwards on the chair, trying to get away from me as fast as possible. I'm sure he was thinking that I was about to explode on him and that he didn't want to be anywhere near me when I did. He couldn't get me out of there fast enough." I chuckled as I shared the experience with Mike.

Being pushed to the limits was no accident. I knew there was something wrong, and I was not going to be ignored any longer. Boundaries had been crossed, and I had made the choice to stand up for myself.

"Good for you," he congratulated me. "Maybe now we will figure this all out."

I was ready for all of this to be over. I had the MRI of my lumbar spine and then waited for my appointment with the neurologist. It had been eight full months since the Spirit had whispered to me as I ascended the hill on that back country road.

I begged Mike to go with me. I knew he was busy, but this was important. And quite honestly, I wanted to know *I* was important. I felt certain that we were going to find the cause of the pain and suffering, and I didn't want to face it on my own. Somehow, I knew that we were finally going to get the answers to the questions we had been asking for so long.

Mike did meet me at that appointment and the next several appointments. Ultimately it took a second MRI, this one of my cervical spine, before the neurologist was confident he had a complete diagnosis.

"You have a bulging disk in your lower back at L5-S1 and a ruptured disk in your neck at C5-6," he said stoically.

Panic tightened my chest as he circled the areas on the MRI, showing us the issues.

"So, what now?" I heard myself whisper timidly. My stomach felt like several hundred kamikaze butterflies had taken flight, and I was staring directly into his deep blue eyes to see if I could surmise any feelings of concern; but, he was as emotional as a block of ice.

"We will surgically remove it," he casually replied, as if it was no big deal—like he was suggesting a trip to the circus or a ride on a Ferris wheel. As if he had heard my thoughts, he confirmed my assessment with a flippant, "I do these all the time." He swung his legs down as he dismounted his chair and, with one step, was standing before me.

Reaching around behind my neck, he gently tilted my head back.

"We will simply make an incision here," he began his surgery dialogue as he drew his finger from the right side of my neck, beginning just below the jawline and moving toward my throat, in a horizontal line.

No, not surgery! I did not see that coming and could feel the panic begin to envelop me. I was trying very hard to hold back the flood waters, but a single tear escaped and rolled slowly down my cheek. Maybe I was naïve, but the thought of surgery had never crossed my mind.

I've never heard of anyone coming out of back surgery without additional problems! Is this going to slow me down even more? What if something happens and I'm forever crippled?

The rest of the appointment and the following eight weeks were a blur, comprised of the surgery at L5-S1, recuperating for six weeks, and then having surgery to remove the ruptured cervical disk.

It was the week before Thanksgiving and there I was, still recovering and learning some serious lessons in humility. Not only did I need assistance to simply roll over in bed every couple of hours, but I required help to the bathroom, into and out of the shower, making meals for my family, and more.

My mom came over several times a week, doing most of the cleaning and laundry. The Relief Society sisters from church graciously brought in meals, and many friends and family came to visit. One day, I was visiting with one of the sisters from church, sharing how mortifying it was to be forced to move so slowly and have everyone doing things for me.

She smiled at me and, with compassion, replied, "Lori, you need to allow us to help you. If you don't, you are taking away blessings from others."

Wow! I have never thought of it that way.

Over the next thirteen months, I did eventually regain my ability to drive myself around to my many doctor's appointments and therapy sessions. The first time I stepped on a treadmill, I didn't last two minutes, but I worked diligently at each of the exercises and sometimes went to the gym twice a day in an effort to improve. It was slow but determined progress.

The day finally came when the neurologist ordered my functional capacity evaluation, a report that would determine my ability going forward.

It had been nearly two years, to the day, since the original accident. I arrived early in the morning, and we began the gamut of tests from walking up and down stairs, lifting, pushing, pulling, and more. After several hours, I was completely exhausted.

A couple of weeks later, Mike and I sat still in the examining room, listening to the neurologist go over my report. My stomach lurched as I heard him say, "No lifting of more than ten pounds repetitively. Part-time work, if you are capable of working at all." As he droned on, all I could hear him saying was, "You won't do this and you won't do that."

My head spinning, I began wondering, *What WILL I be capable of doing? Stop! You are taking everything away from me!* I wanted to scream and barely held myself together through the appointment and the drive home.

It wasn't until Mike and I were discussing the results in our bedroom that it hit me. He was sitting on the edge of the bed when sheer determination consumed me.

Nobody is going to tell me what I can and cannot do!

I resolutely walked over and stood in front of Mike. Tears streamed down my face as I stared into his big brown eyes, put my hands firmly on my hips, reached into the depths of my soul for courage, and announced, "This is NOT acceptable."

This moment, of refusing to believe and act upon someone else's ideas of what I could or would be capable of doing, amounted to a life-defining decision for me. *I* would choose what my abilities and limitations would and would not be.

As you have read, the accident slowed my entire life down, almost to a screeching halt. For someone who moved as quickly and often as I did, the pain of being slowed down regularly competed with the actual physical pain.

Are there circumstances—accidents, losses, or tragedies—that have occurred in your life and forced you to slow down? What physical, emotional, or mental pain is slowing you down, no matter how hard you try to speed your life back up? Are you accepting other's limiting beliefs as your own, or are you choosing to decide for yourself what you are capable of?

"The swerve is not a deviation from the path, but a necessary shift in perspective that leads to new horizons."

Stephen Greenblatt
Author of *The Swerve*

Choice #2

Early the next morning, I dropped Joshua at school and turned toward the gym, which was, ironically, next to the copy store—my original destination the day of the accident now two years behind me.

Wow, has it only been two years? I wondered as I pulled into the parking lot. *Feels like a lifetime since I've felt well.*

The parking lot was nearly full, but I found a spot.

Come on, Lori, you can do this, I told myself as I pulled my achy body out of the car and determinedly walked toward the entrance.

The scent of sweaty bodies and old gym shoes hit my nose at the door, evoking a smelly but sweet memory of the good old days when my boys would play intense soccer games and then remove their stinky soccer cleats on the way home, permeating our vehicle with the foul odor of putrid feet.

Ugh... that was so gross.

Speaking of gross, I thought, catching a glimpse of myself in a mirror against the back wall of the gym. *Even my baggy shirt cannot hide the accumulated layers of fat around my middle, jiggling this way and that as my thighs rub against each other and cause my sweats to rotate back and forth in perfect cadence. And my butt, protruding out like... Oh, I don't want to go there. What happened to that body I worked so hard to maintain— the one that looked great in a pair of shorts?*

The noise and activity of the gym brought me back to the task at hand. Glancing away from the mirror, I noticed a trainer working with a woman on the free weights.

Will my back be strong enough to lift weights again? I glanced back at my reflection for a moment. *Be patient,* I encouraged myself. *One step at a time...*

I stepped onto an elliptical trainer, placed my water bottle in the holder, and set the controls on the lowest possible level. Noticing the woman next to me, I felt intimidated. She was in the zone with beads of sweat forming on her brow, while the machine whirred anew with each downward movement.

Quit worrying about what others think, I coached myself. *She hasn't noticed and besides, why would she care what you do? Now focus!*

Every ounce of my energy was exuded as I urged myself to become stronger and increase my endurance. I fiercely gripped the handles, forcing them back and forth and willing my legs to move faster as I increased the speed for short spurts of time at each interval.

It's only level two! I screamed at myself while wiping drops of sweat with my shirt-sleeve. I wondered if I could endure to the end without passing out. *Just keep moving...*

Thirty, twenty-nine, twenty-eight... counting down the final thirty seconds of the workout, I finally reached zero. Coming slowly to a stop, I grabbed my water and guzzled the rest of the precious liquid. *Congratulations! You made it without dying! Woo hoo!* Barely able to stand, I shuffled to the cleaning spray and snatched a towel to wipe down the machine.

I returned home saturated with sweat, utterly exhausted, and anticipating a shower. The warm spray felt fantastic as it flowed down my aching body. I leaned against the shower wall and closed my eyes.

Mmmm... I want to curl up and go to sleep, right here.

I lingered a few moments longer before reluctantly turning off the soothing water. My legs felt as though they weighed a ton as I hauled them up and over the edge of the tub. Using my last bit of energy, I proceeded to dry off and reached for my usual attire of baggy sweat pants and t-shirt.

Unable to avoid the mirror, I slumped at the sight, wondering if I would ever fit into my normal clothes again. Fifty-seven pounds had adhered themselves to my body since the accident, resisting every attempt to melt them away. Despite my best efforts for months, I had lost a mere four pounds and felt downtrodden. My eyes dropped to the floor in shame just before my stomach growled.

Food!

Unfortunately, eating had become a way to cope with my pent-up emotions. This, combined with my slow metabolism and inability to intensely exercise, was a recipe for disaster. The cascading rolls of fat in my reflection made me nauseous.

I'm so fat and ugly! Why can't I lose this extra weight? I quickly pulled on my t-shirt and turned away. *I'm so tired of struggling with my weight. Here I thought those days were over when I was an active mom and wife, but now I feel like that chubby little kid again!*

As I pulled on my baggy pants, childhood memories flooded my mind.

Staying with Grandma and Grandpa for two weeks was a yearly event that I cherished. One summer shortly after my tenth birthday, Grandma took my sister and me shopping for new dresses. We picked out a cute Holly Hobby patchwork print, which was available in both our sizes, and eagerly headed to the dressing rooms to try them on.

The dress was simple: a bold orange print with splashes of purple and green, and an elastic waist and neckline. I closed the curtain, slipped the garment over my head, and excitedly turned toward the mirror.

Egad! The elastic waist certainly did not enhance my figure and only accentuated my roundness. *I look like a patchwork pumpkin!*

I gingerly stepped out of the dressing room, full of dread. Grandma was busy adjusting my little sister's new dress, which she had tried to put on backwards. She looked so sweet—a perfect little doll.

Grandma looked up and smiled at me. "Well, don't you look cute!"

Taking a deep breath, I edged closer to Grandma and mumbled, "I'm SO fat!"

She leaned over, put her arm around my shoulders, and pulled me lovingly toward her. In her sweet and sincere tone, she said, "Oh sweetie, you are not fat. You are just pleasantly plump," as if that made everything better and being "plump" was a fine thing to be.

Pleasantly plump! I nearly burst into tears but did not wish to cause a scene or, worse, hurt grandma's feelings. I sadly turned away before she noticed the tear rolling down my cheek. The comment was not meant to be hurtful, but to my ten-year-old self, it was a crushing confirmation of what I already knew. I was F... A... T!

Poor Grandma. She had no idea that the brief exchange concerning my weight made an indelible impression, I thought as I finished pulling my pants up. *I never recounted the conversation or felt upset with her; Grandma was simply telling the truth as she saw it, and even at that tender age, I understood and grew to appreciate her honesty.*

The lifelong battle with weight had severely affected my self-image and confidence, and I had constantly monitored every bite in order to maintain a healthy lifestyle, even when I was extremely active before the accident.

Now look at yourself, I chastised, glancing at the mirror. *You are heavier than you have ever been—even heavier than when you were pregnant. What an ugly woman you are!*

Suddenly, I realized that this conversation was going nowhere and stopped it. *STOP beating yourself up*, I chided. *It doesn't fix a thing! Look ahead. You need to swerve around these thoughts and avoid blowing up situations by thinking the worst when you are working so hard to change them.*

I started for the kitchen to find something to eat. Opening the refrigerator, I instantly laid eyes on some tempting leftover bacon.

That is not a lean protein, I sulkily reminded myself. *FINE, I won't eat it!*

I chose a hardboiled egg with some cucumber slices and settled comfortably on the living room couch to devour the healthy snack.

My head nestled into the soft cushions of the sofa when the food was gone.

I really should get going but I am sooooo tired. I closed my eyes. *Surely ten minutes to rest won't hurt. Besides, I deserve it.*

The day was half-gone by the time I awoke.

Crap, I thought, pulling myself off the couch and taking my dishes into the kitchen. *Lunch time. All I do is eat and sleep like a baby. Good grief!*

This pattern became a consistent habit, and before I knew it, the beautiful spring season had arrived.

Exercising on the elliptical machine every morning was grueling work for my body, but I persisted and remained focused on my goals. Unfortunately, in spite of my best efforts, I saw minimal headway in my physical progress and wished I could afford a trainer to help me.

There must be a happy medium between being so thoroughly wiped out and progress, I surmised as I pushed myself on the machine. At this rate, returning to "normal" was going to take a very, very long time and staying motivated was becoming a challenge.

As I increased the resistance of the elliptical from level 2 to level 3, my thoughts drifted to the pioneer trek youth conference in Alcova, Wyoming, that our church was hosting and my assignment as a "Ma" for one of the handcart companies. I worried about being strong enough for the venture since the trip was not for the faint-hearted, requiring arduous walking plus other strenuous duties.

Is it possible for me to be ready by June—only two months away? I wondered, wiping the sweat off my face with a towel.

Increasing my endurance was absolutely imperative because afternoon naps were not part of the conference agenda!

I was determined to improve, so that I would be the help they expected me to be.

No one entirely understands what has transpired since the car accident and the difficulties I face on a daily basis. My mind starts with a list of things to accomplish, but after several small physical chores, exhaustion takes over. I have to listen to my body, because depleting my energy causes additional setback. I have no time for backward momentum.

And with that, I hopped off the machine for the day.

Above and beyond my physical limitations, other challenges wreaked havoc on our small family. These obstacles, like waves, crashed upon us one after the other. Just as we would rise above the water's surface gasping for air, another surge developed, pushing us back under.

When Mike's construction company started to struggle, things became really tough and tight for our little family. As an independent contractor, Mike found it increasingly difficult to purchase individual plots of land. The local housing market had skyrocketed and many subdivisions were being constructed along the Front Range of Colorado. As a result, developers were only selling lots in mass quantities.

"We do not have sufficient capital to invest in group lots." Mike's frustration level was high after another burdensome day. "Only the big contractors with deep pockets can play this game, and I don't know what to do." I could see the wear and tear of this stress in the deep furrows of his brow and the unconscious sighs he let out with each breath. The weight of the burden was evident in the slump of his shoulders as he paced back and forth across the hardwood floor of our living room with its tall coved ceilings and camel-colored walls.

"I understand sweetheart and I am sorry," I said, feeling helpless while wrapping him in a warm bear hug.

What can I do to relieve some of his pressure? I contemplated.

"There's nothing you can do," he replied, reading my mind, "unless you can convince the contractors to sell me one lot at a time."

We tenderly embraced, clinging to each other for dear life and choosing to seek peace and guidance from Heavenly Father through heartfelt prayer, while desperately fighting to keep our family afloat.

Although the answers were not immediate nor complete and would require a huge leap of faith and trust, we felt inspired to close the construction company and sell our home, as the first two steps to stop the hemorrhage of money that was depleting our bank account.

The one beacon of light during those turbulent months was the marriage of our son, Chris, to his beautiful bride, Candie. What a memorable and heartwarming occasion. The family gathered to celebrate their joyous springtime wedding, and we welcomed the distraction. However, as the couple drove away to begin their new life in Branson, Missouri, an emptiness swelled inside of me and uncertainty hovered like a stormy cloud.

Money was tight as Mike completed his remaining contracts, and I was thankful that my wholesale foods business and scrapbooking classes kept food on the table and covered our necessary expenses. The budget no longer afforded "wants," which regrettably included my gym membership.

How am I going to continue to improve? I stewed, working myself into a frazzle one day as I noticed that it felt like my strength was declining. I lacked the certainty to maintain my exercise program and steady improvement without the use of the gym. Sinking with despair and feeling overwhelmed, I longed for the ability to believe in myself. The lack of funds for a gym membership had become an easy excuse to postpone my physical recovery.

YOU have to do SOMETHING! I scolded myself one morning in the same living room where my husband had paced about his limitations. *The sun is shining, and it is a beautiful day, so get off your butt and go for a walk. Stop feeling sorry for yourself and GET BUSY!*

I feared I would fall into the dark abyss, never to return, if I did not immediately modify my focus. The screen door slammed defiantly behind me as I stomped out to navigate our twelve acres of land, circumventing the destructive mode I was in. The clean fresh air was a healing balm to my troubled soul and replaced my fear and frustration with hope. Raising my head, I triumphantly strode another lap around the property, enjoying the exercise.

During my long walk through the cornfields, I contemplated my recovery. Walking was beneficial, yet I needed something more intense.

Workout videos! Surely, they will make a difference!

Bursting through the front door, I went straight to the video cabinet and dug out the exercise tapes buried under countless children's movies.

There's no better time than the present, I assured myself, inserting a tape into the VCR.

Five minutes in, I collapsed onto the floor, aching and breathing heavily.

Whew, that's all I can do today, I groaned. *I don't remember these tapes being so difficult.* I had not done the workouts since the car accident and I was drained. *Where is the resilience I used to have? What am I going to do? Will I have to accept that this is the way it will be?*

The questions bombarded me while I laid flat on the floor, trying to gather my strength. Eventually, my resolve to be whole again forced me to choose to sit up and fight back.

NO! I am going to figure this out and somehow, I will win!

Over the next few weeks, my progress continued to steadily improve with every walk and workout video. Mike was out of town, and I stayed busy preparing to sell the house. I enlisted friends to help with repairs that I could not do alone, and they happily assisted with painting and other sundry tasks.

Allowing others the opportunity to serve does not mean you are weak, I humbly acknowledged.

Before long, a "For Sale" sign stood proudly in the front yard, and I was eager for Mike to arrive home and see what I had accomplished over the two weeks he was away.

"Hi, Babe!" I answered the phone enthusiastically when I saw his number.

"Did you decide to kick me to the curb?" Mike sternly questioned. I could hear the laughter in his voice and played along.

"No, why would you say that?" I shot back. Having completed my errands, I was almost home and could not wait to see him!

"Well, I came home early only to discover a 'For Sale' sign standing in the yard and my key no longer opens the door. Everything has been done and you are nowhere to be found," he teased.

"I'm closer than you think," I retorted, driving past the grove of trees which hid me from view and pulling promptly into the driveway. I threw open the door and hastened toward him. He smiled, gently scooped me up, and slathered me with kisses.

"Missed you," we chimed in together, laughing and teasing about whether or not I would allow him inside.

By the time June arrived, I had grown stronger and could finish generous portions of the workout videos and long walks without feeling spent.

A huge improvement! I cheerfully congratulated myself with a smile and was ecstatic when I obtained permission from the doctor to go on the trek, despite the stern warning not to do any lifting, pushing, or pulling.

"Yes, I did it!" I exclaimed enthusiastically, enjoying the view of the hundred plus youth before me, loading up their handcarts and taking off on this adventure with their new "families" for the week. "I have made myself strong enough for this, and it is going to be fun."

Unfortunately, even with all the extra strength, sleeping in a tent and walking five miles or more daily next to a hand cart proved to be extremely taxing on my body. Unexpected emotions surfaced as I stood aside, unable to assist each time the kids encountered a large hill or tough obstacle.

I refuse to be a mere observer the rest of my life, I determined, brushing away tears for the umpteenth time, as I watched the kids struggle to keep the handcart going without my help. Although the trek set me back physically, I had successfully attained my goal and believed it was the beginning of better things to come.

The house sold in midsummer, just before the bank was to start foreclosure proceedings. Oh, what a relief! I was grateful for the sale, but quietly wondered where we were going to live.

"It would be great if we could stay in the house for a few months until we figure things out," I commented to our realtor.

"That would be helpful," Mike agreed, "since we don't have a place to rent."

"I don't think the buyer is in a hurry," the realtor responded. "I may be able to negotiate your move-out date." A few days later, he called to inform us that a six-month lease had been approved.

"Woo hoo!" I exclaimed as I hung up the phone, giving Mike a high-five, then solemnly adding, "Heavenly Father knows our struggles. I know better, but was beginning to think He didn't care." I gave Mike a gentle squeeze, went to our bedroom, and closed the door.

This was a close call. Had the house not sold, the fallout from foreclosure would have blown up our financial future for years to come. Dropping to my knees beside the bed, I prayed; *Heavenly Father, I thank Thee for Thy goodness and tender mercies, and please forgive my doubting heart.* I paused, wondering what I had ever done to deserve Heavenly Father's blessings. *We need Thy help, Father, and can't do this without Thee. Please help us to have faith and know where Thou wouldst have us go. I love Thee and want to follow Thy plan for us. In Jesus name, Amen.*

A warm sensation filled me, and I felt Heavenly Father's arms wrapped tightly around me. My prayer was heard and I knew He was beside me.

Mike and I continued to pray and seek for answers while company operations closed, funds ran low, and time ticked away. After contemplating our options, we chose to move forward in faith and decided that if Mike could secure work, we would relocate to Branson, Missouri.

With only a duffle bag of clothes and a trailer full of tools, Mike was ready to go. Joshua and I would stay in Colorado until a job and living arrangements could be procured. Early one crisp fall morning, following lots of hugs, kisses, and promises to be careful, he pulled out of the driveway and turned east toward Branson.

Heavenly Father, we are going completely on faith. Please protect my sweetheart, I prayed as Mike's truck disappeared over the hill and into the rising sun.

Our new adventure had begun!

I gave Joshua a reassuring squeeze and cheerfully said, "It's just you and me, Buddy."

His dad's absences due to work had been rough on him and the separation of our family was unsettling.

"Yeah, guess so," he muttered noncommittally.

Complicating his myriad of teenage feelings was the fear of leaving best friends behind and beginning anew in a strange high school, hundreds of miles away. He was miserable and imparted his disdain at every opportunity.

As he stood there, staring at the horizon where his dad's car disappeared, I felt a growing ache in the pit of my stomach. I knew how hard this was.

Between kindergarten and the sixth grade, I had attended five elementary schools in three different towns and hated starting over each time my family moved. I was especially shy and lacked the boldness to easily acquire new friends; and adding to my insecurity was the fact that most of my clothes were hand-me-downs from my cousins who were petite, like my sister. Each morning, I crammed my "pleasantly plump" body into their pint-sized clothes while avoiding anything with buttons or zippers for fear they would pop open. I desired a true friend, but was awkward and never genuinely fit in with my peers.

Understanding this moment would not last much longer, I reached out and gave Joshua a hug and a few encouraging words before he was off to wallow in his discontent. He seemed to toss my words aside as if I could not possibly understand his pain.

I understand, I mouthed as my mind slipped back to one particularly horrifying day of trying to make new friends.

The worst part of my school day was always recess. Out of sight and earshot of the playground monitor, my schoolmates either totally ignored me or mercilessly teased me. Outside of the classroom, I felt exposed and vulnerable and would stay inside and read whenever I was allowed.

I was surprised and delighted one day when two girls in my class asked me to join them for afternoon recess.

Do they really want to be MY friends? I wondered in amazement. The girl in charge had been proudly displaying her shiny new go-go boots, which I had been admiring the entire morning. The only pair of boots I owned were big, old, red galoshes worn over my shoes whenever it rained. I happily accepted their invitation, anticipating the fun.

The recess bell finally rang, and we ventured out the door, skipping and chattering to the far end of the playground. I was enjoying myself and basking in their invitation when their real motivation was revealed.

One girl stood with her hands behind her back while the other girl looked at me with a big grin and said, "Close your eyes, open your mouth, and get ready for a BIG SURPRISE!"

A silent scheme passed between them as they glanced at each other and giggled. Desperately wanting to believe that we could be friends, I willingly closed my eyes and opened wide. A moment later, my mouth was jammed full of white dandelion puffs, and I heard laughter from every direction. My eyes popped open as I spewed seed pods and saw many of my classmates gathered around for the entertainment at my expense.

I was mortified and keenly aware that friendship was not on anyone's agenda.

The bell rang and I was left alone with my shattered heart. Spitting, choking, and sobbing, I slowly made my way back to class and heaped more shame upon myself.

How could you fall for that, Stupid? They are not interested in you, Dumb Fat Girl!

I secretly hoped the next move would be soon.

I don't need friends, I numbly decided.

Looking back toward the rising sun, I thought about saying goodbye to family and friends and starting over. This time, it would be hard. I had developed genuine friendships during the past seven years and was fearful that I would never again experience the closeness I felt with those who had accepted me.

Making friends is easy for Joshua, I reasoned. *With his vibrant personality, charm, and big brown eyes, he shouldn't have any problems.* I chuckled as I headed inside to get on with my day, musing about how his charisma had worked on me more than once.

The days passed slowly while Mike and I were separated, and I oscillated between emotions of failure and determination. I buoyed my spirits by completing more reps of a particularly difficult exercise, fulfilling my to-do list, or taking final orders for my wholesale foods business. I missed having Mike home and anticipated our evening chats. As I crawled into bed each night, I took comfort in the thought of knowing we were one day closer to being together.

He found work, and one evening shortly before Thanksgiving, he called and asked, "How would you feel about cutting expenses by sharing a house with Chris and Candie?"

"What do the kids think?" I inquired excitedly, my heart skipping a beat at the thought.

"Willing if you are," Mike replied quickly.

"I would love to be together as a family again!" I exclaimed.

A small house was rented in Branson, and Mike and the kids prepared to move. I also needed to begin the rigorous task of packing since Mike was going to arrive in Colorado on Christmas Eve. After spending Christmas with the family, he would load the truck and return to Branson the following day. Joshua would stay with me in Colorado until January in order to finish the school semester and allow me one final "hurrah" at girl's winter camp before moving to our new home.

Might as well jump in, I thought one chilly morning while heading to the basement with tape, scissors, notebook, and a sharpie. I knew the job would be challenging since lifting anything heavier than a gallon of milk repetitively was still immensely difficult. After an hour of working, I was spent and flopped onto a bed, stared at the ceiling, and announced, "Break time!" I realized with a deep sigh that the only way I could manage this move was to pack, rest, pack, rest. Joshua's responsibility would be to stack the filled boxes against the wall.

He'll be thrilled, I smirked.

A barrage of unexpected emotions and memories overtook me as I began sorting my craft room. *Oh, how different this time of year is for me now.* Tears welled and made it hard for me to see what I was doing.

Prior to my injuries, I would be preparing for a host of local craft shows as well as my own small show in our home. Through my tears, I laughed at the thought that I was included in an elite class of women who requested power tools for gifts. I loved crafting.

Up until the year after the accident, as soon as the kids returned to school every fall, the fun would begin! I loved the sound of the scroll saw, the hum of the drill spinning away, and the smell of saw dust in the air as I merrily cut out the wooden pieces. The excitement of painting and creating a final project that people would use to decorate their homes filled me with pride and joy.

"Not Christmas music *already*," was a regularly groaned phrase, as my two boys relentlessly teased me about my early preparations and holiday music playing in September. I always ignored their comments and cheerfully continued with my creations.

And now, I was exhausted and wept big tears of frustration, longing for what had been as I stuffed carton after carton with wooden cut outs, sandpaper, paints, and various assortments of beads, ribbons, stencils, and other craft supplies that had not been used in nearly two years.

A sea of boxes was left in my wake, and I was about to enlist Joshua's help when he hollered down the stairs, "Hey, Mom, I'm hungry!"

Perfect timing. I could not handle any more emotional memories and was happy to stop and promise Joshua dinner after the boxes were stacked.

As each day progressed, my roller coaster of emotions resulted in tears, tears, and more tears as I packed up the contents of our lives and was reminded of what I used to enjoy. Simple objects such as pictures, volley and soccer balls, journals, water bottles, hiking boots, or cake decorating tools induced waves of sadness.

One evening while looking at piles of boxes stacked high against the walls, I allowed myself a very quick celebration of my achievements with a hearty pat on the back. Still, a sense of panic cascaded over me like a waterfall as I glanced around the room and realized there was still much to do. Joshua was unhappy about my constant reminders to help and his persistent grumbling wore on me, adding to my crankiness and desire to do everything myself.

Party time is over. Get back to work!

Moving day was rapidly approaching and everything had to be ready by the time Mike arrived in town on Christmas Eve.

I'm never going to finish this alone, I thought and resolved to recruit some extra hands. *It shouldn't be this hard!*

Again, with the help of others throughout the next week, I was tossing the last few items into a bin when Mike appeared in the doorway and bellowed over the Christmas music, "Anybody home?"

The sound of his voice instantly filled me with joy and relief. Dropping everything, I hurriedly maneuvered toward him through the maze, nearly plowing him down as I threw my arms around him.

"I'm happy to see you too!" he laughed as I snuggled against his chest.

We spent a lovely Christmas day at my mom's home, reveling in our last Colorado holiday with extended family. Before we knew it, Christmas was over and the truck was loaded. Joshua and I again stood alone on the porch, waving to Mike and a family friend as they vanished beyond the horizon.

Two weeks later, Joshua and I bid our goodbyes to family and friends, loaded the car with our remaining belongings, and began the lengthy drive to Branson, nearly a thousand miles away.

"So long, Colorado," I tenderly called out, watching the familiar scenery disappear in my rearview mirror and anticipating what the future would hold.

The beautiful rocks and hills of Branson were a most welcome sight. Mike was anxiously waiting and greeted us warmly when we finally arrived. Moving had taken a toll on my body, and several days passed before I had sufficient energy to tackle the mountain of boxes in the garage. When I was able, Mike and Joshua brought our belongings into the house, and I spent the days unpacking and organizing the contents into the tiny 900 square feet we had agreed to share.

Settled in our home, I was ready for a routine and was relieved when I soon made friends with our sweet neighbor, who was also our landlord. We enjoyed walking together and helping each other overcome obstacles, as she had also been in a serious accident and could understand many of my challenges. I felt as if Heavenly Father placed her directly in my path.

Early summer brought yet another change when Chris accepted a new apprenticeship in computer programming, which required him and Candie to return to Colorado. The house felt lonely without them, and I especially missed my heart-to-heart talks with Chris and Candie's creative flair and female companionship.

Joshua was now fourteen and, unbeknownst to me, he had begged a couple from our ward to give him a job on the lighting and sound crew at one of the many live theaters in the area. They also owned a hotel near the venue, and I was surprised when I was offered a front desk position that would coordinate with Joshua's schedule. I explained my physical limitations and wearily agreed to a six-hour shift on Monday, Wednesday, and Friday evenings, plus every other Saturday morning. My additional income would definitely help our budget, and Joshua's new job was a great opportunity to teach responsibility and budgeting skills.

By the end of each shift, I was dead tired. Oftentimes, my speech became slurred and unorganized, like I was throwing the words in the air and having them randomly shower down in discombobulated gibberish. Sleeping most of the day during my time off was the only way I managed to have enough strength to satisfy my assigned duties on the days I did work.

Despite these difficulties, I considered the endeavor a blessing. I slowly increased my hours over the next several months, as heaven knew we needed extra funds to combat the endless bombardment of bills from the closure of Mike's company. Even though I still had to listen to my body and be cautious, my stamina gradually improved.

Then, it was Christmas time again, and the busy theater season was coming to a close. Chris and Candie were coming for the holiday, and while contentedly wrapping presents, I reflected upon the last year of my life.

I had made significant improvements since the previous December, when I could not lift the moving boxes or work for more than an hour or two without rest.

Heavenly Father's handiwork is evident—inspiration to move to Branson, my employment, church callings working with the youth, and the list goes on. Hmmm. Maybe there really are no accidents.

I was humbled at these thoughts and felt His love and the spirit of the season enveloping me like a warm blanket.

Carefully pulling the paper tight around the next package, I wondered at the events that had transpired since the accident, nearly three years earlier. *Those many months of arguing with doctors, different therapy modalities, MRIs, surgeries, rehab, and the functional capacity evaluation, not to mention nearly losing the house, being separated from Mike for months, and then the packing and moving across the country.* Those were stressful times, and I was overcome with gratitude and amazement at the physical and spiritual strides I had made as I swerved around each challenge and obstacle, maneuvering my way toward recovery.

Sitting on the floor for this long would not have been possible, I noted as I tied a pretty ribbon in place and topped it with a bow.

Pushing myself up into a kneeling position, I placed the package under the tree and stretched for a moment to get the blood again flowing. My body was beginning to twinge, but I had one final gift, and then all the packages would be ready. Choosing a smiling snowman print, I slipped back into my reflections of the past.

Baby steps. Forward progress, that's the key, I surmised. *And what progress I have made!* My goals were challenging and often times required reevaluation and drawing a new line in the sand, making additional smaller steps of advancement in order to reach my aspirations.

I excitedly wondered what incredible adventures Heavenly Father had in store for me and could not envision the self-confidence and unimaginable courage I would obtain with each new and difficult step outside my comfort zone.

This phase of my journey was about swerving around the many obstacles—spiritual, emotional, and financial—that could have blown up in my life. Much like swerving to avoid the woman on the road the day of the accident, my choices to navigate around these obstacles kept me from exploding and/or imploding with fear, anxiety, and pain.

What obstacles have occurred in your life—spiritually, emotionally, financially, relationally, etc.—and are causing you to swerve, change your course of action, or draw a new line in the sand? Are you watching and looking for opportunities to change the situation and swerve onto a new path, where you can regain some control?

How do you swerve? Of course, I don't mean the kind where you avoid the obstacle *and* the emotions it brings up, but the kind of swerving that helps you to navigate around it all with more ease. I used prayer, honest communication, and movement to swerve around some of my obstacles, but I know there are many ways people navigate these situations.

"The climb might be tough and challenging, but the view is worth it. There is a purpose for that pain; you just can't always see it right away."

Victoria Arlen

ESPN Personality and Former American Paralympian Swimmer

Choice #3

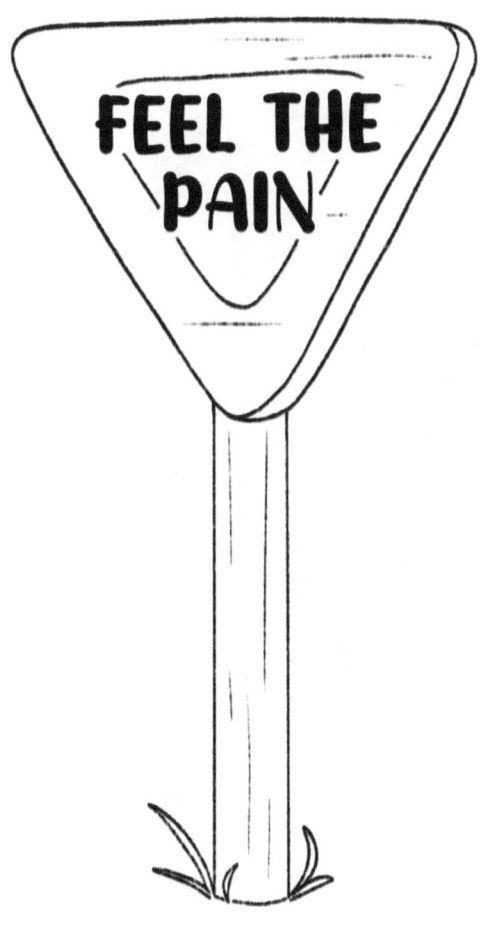

My stamina and fortitude continued to improve as each month came and went. Moving from my shorter night shift to an eight to ten-hour day shift gave me more options in the tasks I was assigned. I enjoyed scheduling group events at the theater and booking bus tours staying in the hotel. Inputting all the rooms was like playing a huge game of Tetris as I tried to keep the groups together in and amongst other guests who would be arriving or leaving on different days.

My favorite aspect of the job, however, was the relationships we enjoyed with the guests. The manager and I would greet the buses as they arrived at the hotel, their anticipation for the adventures that awaited them vibrating through the air. Of course, as they would come and go throughout their stay, they would engage us in conversation. Many of our regulars would come every few months and, at some point during their stay, would congregate in the breakfast area—only a few steps away from the front desk, to play cards and banter with us as they enjoyed each other's company.

I'd also started doing the bookkeeping and helping with payroll, proofing the advertising, updating the online bookings, and handling some of the not-so-pleasant issues that inevitably arose.

One of the first big ventures outside of my comfort zone came when a year-end review was scheduled with my boss. With all of the responsibility I had taken on throughout the year, I felt that if I were to continue working the following season, I was due a raise. In fact, I was praying desperately that it would be his idea to increase my pay. When I confided in Mike about this desire, we brainstormed ways to ask and roleplayed how to handle each possible situation.

Mike made it seem simple as he pretended to be my boss, smiling widely from across the kitchen table, "Will you stay on for the next season?"

I blushed at this game as I attempted to keep my thoughts from scrambling and answered, "Well, I have taken on several additional tasks this year and feel that I am worth more."

"List out the things you have taken on," Mike said, his brown eyes dancing encouragingly at me. "Be brave. He may not realize all that you are doing."

Shoulders sagging with inferiority, I responded, "But I feel so strange asking for more money. Like I am begging."

Mike came over and gave me a gentle but reassuring squeeze and kissed the top of my head. "You are not begging," he coached me, putting his hands on my shoulders and continuing with pride, "You work hard, and you deserve a raise."

After several more tries and figuring out exactly how much I required to stay, I determinedly promised that if a raise was not offered, I would ask.

The next morning, butterflies were zipping around in my stomach as I contemplated, for the hundredth time, how this would all transpire.

Am I being too bold? Am I really good enough to deserve a raise?

The time for my meeting was drawing near and self-doubt was rearing its ugly head once more. Just as my boss walked through the front door of the small hotel, the thought again surfaced: *What if he says no?*

That's when I heard Mike's calm and gentle voice in my mind, "Be brave. You are worth it."

I only hoped my boss felt the same way.

"Ready for our meeting," he warmly greeted me, a wide smile spreading across his face.

I smiled in return and made my way to the table where he had comfortably plopped into a seat. The breakfast table was only a few feet away from the front desk, where my co-worker and customers could easily overhear our conversation, which left me feeling exposed and even more self-conscious. We conversed about my performance during the previous year and at the end of our conversation, he asked, "Would you be willing to continue on this coming year?"

While this was good news, meaning he was happy with my performance, there was no indication that there would be a raise.

I fumbled with my words as I scraped together the courage from the far reaches of my soul.

Be brave. You are worth it, I told myself as he further inquired, "Oh, and would you also be willing to take on additional duties?"

I paused. Still no indication of a raise.

Just go for it! I told myself.

Finally, I found my voice. "I am willing to continue as long as there is an increase in pay," I stated boldly, squaring my shoulders for the impact of what I thought was coming.

He sat riveted and looked at me with a surprised expression that made me cringe inwardly as I waited for the repercussions.

Have I spoken out of turn?

He gained his composure and asked indifferently, "What do you think you deserve?"

What do I deserve? The question hung in the air. Ever since I was a child, I felt worth very little. A dark cloud of fear began to envelope me and my father's face replaced the face of my boss. Suddenly, I was yanked back through time.

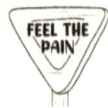

Exasperated with the constant arguing, I exploded, "*/$!#%&%*#!"

I was sixteen years old, and Dad and I had been arguing for years about my friends, school, church, house rules, curfew, my job. You name it. We argued about it. This day was no different. I felt as if I never did anything right in his eyes!

My friends were never good enough, my grades were never high enough (I got my first A- on a spelling test in second grade and was grounded for a week), my room was a pig sty. Okay, that was probably true; but that aside, I was tired of being treated as though I didn't have a voice or an opinion that mattered. And, after sixteen years of it, I snapped and screamed at my father.

My dad was momentarily frozen by my outburst. Knowing his philosophies of "spare the rod, spoil the child" and that "children should be seen and not heard," I took advantage of the few nano seconds I had before the shock wore off, and he inflicted that painful teaching upon me.

I did the only thing I could think of—I turned tail and ran. I tore up the stairs, two and three at a time, out the front door, not caring that the screen door slammed behind me, and toward my car faster than I had ever run in my life.

As he slammed through the door screaming and yelling at me, I covered the last few yards and dove into my 1967 Volkswagen bug, locking both doors in one sweeping move. Dad was nearly to the driveway when I realized my windows were down. Grabbing the handle, I began cranking the window up as rapidly as I could, but I was not fast enough.

Before the window had reached a quarter of the way, Dad had tried the door. Finding it locked added fuel to his already roaring rage; and he reached through the window, grabbed a solid handful of my hair, and jerked me partway out the window as his other hand unlocked the door. He extricated me out of the car and dragged me up the sidewalk by my hair toward the house as I kicked and screamed, "LET ME GO!!"

Across the street, a police car was parked in the driveway.

Maybe our neighbor will hear me and come running out to see what is going on.

But no—no one ever came outside. I was doomed.

I cannot let him get me into the house and close the door. I know what he is capable of.

I put my hands out to keep him from pulling me in. I figured I had nothing left to lose and fought with all my might. Another failed attempt as he yanked so hard that we both fell to the entryway floor, and I found myself at the bottom of the heap, with my tiny pinky throbbing painfully. "You broke my finger!"

It was then that Mom stepped in for the first time I could recall and kicked him in the privates, doing the only thing she could think of to get him off of me. Several hours later and after much "discussion," Mom was finally allowed to take me to the emergency room.

The nurse listened politely as Mom explained that I had been "wrestling" with my dad, and then requested that my mom follow her out of the room. I could see them standing just outside the door but could not hear their conversation. The nurse scowled and marched back through the door, took me down to x-ray, and then returned me to the examination room. Upon looking at the films, a quick diagnosis was reached. My finger was indeed broken—so badly that pins would be required to repair the break. I was scheduled for surgery the following week.

Dad was out of town on a business trip that week, and missed out on the consequences I was suffering at his hand. A few days after my surgery, I was sitting on the couch with my arm elevated, looking at the classified ads in the newspaper, when Mom arrived home from work.

Hitting the threshold, she instantly sensed that something was wrong. "What are you doing?" she asked, worry evident in her tone.

"Just looking for a place to rent," I responded nonchalantly, pulling the paper up so I didn't have to see her face.

I barely finished the sentence before she was standing next to me slapping the paper downward with panic in her voice, "You CAN'T move out! You are not old enough!"

Moving the paper aside, I looked directly into her eyes and boldly replied in a calm, but stern voice, "You can either help me and know where I am, or you don't help me and I'll do it anyway. Doesn't matter to me either way. I'm not staying here anymore!"

Hurt passed through my mother's eyes, but I had to take care of me this time. I had no more to give, and I knew something had to change, or all the heartache and pain was going to destroy me.

I had made up my mind, and there was no turning back. I was tired of feeling like a failure. I wanted to be loved and appreciated for who I was and all that I contributed. I was tired of being told to jump and having to ask, "How high?" on the way up. I had reached my fill and there was no consoling me. I was done!

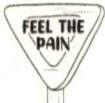

The memory faded, and I found myself staring wide-eyed at my boss. Hoping I had not been "gone" too long and before fear enveloped me, I blurted out the number Mike and I had discussed that would amount to a 17% raise. I was not the same invalid they had initially hired at near minimum wage.

I sat in the silence, afraid to breathe, as he thought about my request. Then, he nonchalantly said, "I think we can make that work," smiled broadly, shook my hand, and thanked me for staying on. As quickly as he had arrived, he was out the door and on to his next task.

I sat still, giving my mind a moment to absorb what had just happened. I was stunned.

Wow, that was not nearly as difficult as I had antici-pated. No arguing. No fighting. No negotiating. Imagine that. He thought I was worth it.

What a huge boost to my self-confidence. Excitement started to bubble up inside of me.

What are these new sensations I'm feeling? I could hardly wait to go home and tell Mike what had just transpired.

I guess all I had to do was choose to speak up and let him know what I have been thinking and wanting.

With the increase in my wages and extra hours, we were able to pay down a good portion of the debt remaining from Colorado. Now with our combined income and my good credit, we purchased an older home east of Branson. Finally, back into a house of our own. Time to party!

Unfortunately, the party energy was short-lived.

I was feeling pretty good about life and the slow-but-steady progress I was making until a few weeks later when a letter from my attorney arrived, stating that it was time for my deposition for the car accident. I was to return to Colorado at the end of May. While reading the letter, feelings of panic tightened my chest and then my shoulders and throat.

What am I going to do?

While my stamina had improved and allowed me longer work days, and I continued to exercise, I was a long way from being whole. I still spent time resting here or there, and the pain was still unbearable at times, especially when sitting or standing for great lengths of time. I did not feel up to driving the 850 miles back to Colorado, let alone dealing with the attorneys. I had worked hard to get this far and was nervous to the point of physical nausea at the thought of dredging up all the memories I had worked incredibly hard to move past.

With no way for Mike to leave town and the kids no longer living in Branson, I wondered who might have time to make the trip with me. Fortunately, my mom and my stepfather had moved to Branson the previous summer, so I called Mom, hoping she would have the flexibility to make the trip with me.

I was elated when she said, "Yes, I would be happy to go with you." Relief flowed through my body as I hung up the phone, plopped myself into the chair, and cried.

This is silly, I thought. *Why am I getting so emotional? I didn't do anything wrong. I will just go and tell my side of the story.*

Mom and I left early the day before the deposition. Having to get out every couple of hours to stretch turned a long drive into an arduous trip. I arrived in Colorado exhausted, greeted the kids, ate dinner, and headed straight for bed, knowing I would need all the strength and energy I could muster for the following day's activities.

I awoke the next morning feeling rested but very nervous. Having never been through a deposition before, I was unsure what to expect.

I turned into the parking lot of a new business complex. Finding the correct suite number, we parked in a space nearby and apprehensively headed for the large wooden entrance. My heart was nearly beating through my chest with mounting anxiety. Walking toward the front desk, I surveyed the pristine white walls with thick, heavily framed pictures evenly spaced around the room. I waited for the receptionist to acknowledge me before attempting to give her my name and the reason for my presence. She smiled stiffly, before greeting us warmly. and then led us down a hallway lined with additional paintings to an oversized wooden door where she knocked. Waiting a brief moment, she opened the door to a room with several chairs surrounding a long table. Pointing to the small refrigerator in the corner of the room, she told us to help ourselves to beverages, nodded knowingly toward the people already seated at the table, and then excused herself and closed the door behind her.

I felt as though I had just been escorted into the lion's den where several ravenous beasts were staring hungrily toward me, contemplating who would start the feeding frenzy.

Heavenly Father, please give me the strength and the right words.

I found the eyes of my attorney first. He was sitting calmly at the end of the table with two additional attorneys, who represented both defendants (the garbage truck driver and the older lady in the car), the person facilitating the deposition, and the woman responsible for recording all that was said.

We exchanged pleasantries and the spokesman leading the deposition inquired snidely as to who I had brought with me. I explained, as they motioned for both of us to be seated, that my mom had graciously come to help me with the fourteen-hour drive from Branson the previous day and was here for moral support.

Any hopes of this being an easy or quick process flew directly out the window as they informed us about the deposition process and ended with the statement that my mom would be allowed to stay as long as she remained quiet. One outburst and she would have to leave.

Wow. Straight and to the point, I see.

I took a deep breath when my attorney asked if I was ready.

"Ready as I will ever be," I nervously surmised and attempted to make myself comfortable in the large leather chair, legs dangling, unable to reach the floor.

Given the okay to begin, the man doing the deposition reminded me that *everything* was being recorded.

No kidding, I thought as the click, click, click of the recorder began its steady cadence, which would continue through the next several hours while she recorded every question asked as well as each of my answers, sighs, and questions.

The questions started slowly and friendly enough. What was my name and date of birth? Did I know why I was there? Was I on any medications? What was my husband's name and my children's names and ages? Which college had I attended, and what degree was I going for?

"A two-year accounting degree," I responded.

Then it started.

"Okay. And why didn't you finish?"

"Because I went through a divorce and my oldest son, who was around three at the time, was terribly sick. I needed to be there to take care of him," I curtly responded.

Quickly, the banter began. It came almost rapid fire, and he often asked the same question multiple ways.

Is he just trying to see if I will change my answer? What difference does it make that I finished college or not? It doesn't make me a liar.

Eventually, I was asked to "paint them a picture" of what I saw and what happened in the accident as I came up over the hill. I described the accident scene from start to finish, ending with my car's blown tire, launching through the air and the landing, where I became stuck in the soft dirt on the side of the road. When I finished, he questioned why I chose the ditch.

Unbelievable, I thought. *As if I had a choice about where I landed, while flying through the air?*

We went over and over every detail. How far into the turn was the garbage truck? Which entrance did he come out of? Was he mid-turn or had he completed the turn? Which lane was he in?

When I could not remember whether it was the second or third entrance into the subdivision, he questioned me again and again from different angles to try to "help" me remember. All this did was frustrate me more. I could not remember, and frankly, I did not care which entrance it was or whether he was partway through a turn or had completed it.

What does this have to do with the lady who nearly hit me?

After several questions concerning the semi-truck driver at the bottom of the hill, I became agitated over not recalling what color the truck was or knowing exactly the distance his truck was from me. Appearing delighted at my frustration, he returned to the garbage truck and started over again.

When we finally got to the car that nearly hit me, he asked, "Where was the white car at that point in time?"

"I never saw the white car until I turned back from glancing to my left at the garbage truck. When I swung my head to look straight ahead, I saw her right in my lane," I responded.

He seemed to be enjoying this cat and mouse game. "Okay. Do you know where that white car had been prior to you seeing it?"

How the hell am I supposed to know where the white car was if I didn't see it until it was right in front of my face?!?! I wanted to scream but I simply responded, "No."

"Can you tell where it would have been?" he persisted, staring at me as if daring me to take the bait and venture a guess.

My mind was swirling, and I wanted to yell, *Asked and answered! Ugh, enough already!*

This line of questioning continued, and I became more and more flustered until he finally asked if I would like to draw it on a piece of paper. I drew the cars and trucks as boxes and the incessant questioning continued.

"Looking at this drawing again," he droned, "are you sure the vehicles are in their correct positions?"

"I'm not sure on the semi, as I previously stated, but I am about the other two and myself," I responded wondering when this would end.

"Are you certain the garbage truck was in the turn lane?" he pushed.

"Yes, I do remember seeing him turn out of the subdivision and into the turn lane because he had plenty of room between him and the semi-truck," I answered with a fair amount of annoyance in my voice, as I wiggled in my seat. Sitting for so long without a break was tough enough, but this incessant badgering was draining my energy. My back begged me to stand, move, or somehow find a more comfortable position.

"Where was the car that you nearly collided with?" He could tell I was uncomfortable, but did not seem to care, as he persisted in trying to trip me up.

Leaning forward, I pointed to the rectangle on the paper I had drawn to indicate her car.

"Are you sure?" he mockingly replied. "How can you be so sure that her position is correct?"

It was at this point my mom could bite her tongue no longer. She walked out of the room and I blew a gasket. "How could I be sure?" I barked, slamming my fist on the table. "Let's see. Maybe it was the fact that I could see the expression on her face and the terror in her eyes because she was so close to me!" I exploded.

Two hours later, I felt exasperated and exhausted, beat down, and not sure that I remembered anything correctly. The constant questioning of every detail and every answer I gave made me feel like I had just done nine rounds with a heavy-weight boxer. Even my attorney stepped in a couple of times, asking about the line of questioning.

I left the room feeling a heaviness—a burden—as if I had been the one who had caused the accident, leaving mass destruction in my wake, instead of the victim who had spent the last three and a half years trying to put the fragmented pieces of her body and life back together.

Mom hugged me as soon as I walked into the hallway. "I'm sorry. I just couldn't stay," she apologized as she pulled away and walked with me to the door. "I wanted to yell at them for hurling accusations at you! I knew that if I opened my mouth, they would throw me out, and I didn't want to be any trouble."

"It's okay, Mom," I assured as we reached the car and flopped into our seats. My endurance had improved significantly over the past eighteen months; but the strain of a fourteen-hour car ride, along with the stress of going through this deposition, was taking its toll. "Just please, take me home."

Looking around the dinner table that evening, staring into the faces of my children and mom, I reaffirmed my love and gratitude for each of them.

Thank you, Heavenly Father, for surrounding me with people who love and care about me!

Before going to bed, I called Mike and told him about my adventure. Feeling badly about being so far away, he said, "They're just lucky I wasn't there! I would have beaten them up for you!"

I laughed gently, appreciating his chivalry. "I love you and can't wait to be home!"

"I'll see you Sunday," he replied, blowing me a kiss before he hung up the phone.

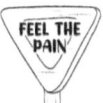

I returned to work, happy the tour season had begun. Welcoming buses and the comradery I felt with the guests helped take my mind off the deposition and the upcoming mitigation.

I had to make yet another trip back to Colorado for the mitigation process in November. With no way to tell whether the garbage truck driver or the lady was at fault, my attorney advised me to settle out of court, especially since she only had a liability policy. In that final meeting, they agreed to pay my medical bills and give me a small amount in case another surgery became necessary. I, in return, agreed that I would not file another claim for additional money should further surgery be required.

Shortly after Christmas, I opened the mailbox to find the small settlement from my accident. After the attorney took his portion, we used the remainder to pay the last few outstanding bills from Colorado. I was not thrilled with the settlement, but I was relieved to have the entire process over.

I was tired of reliving the painful memories and ready to complete my total healing process and move on with life.

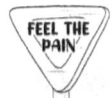

Returning to Branson and being back at work was a great feeling, although I could not help but feel that there was something more I could do. I wanted to use my brain and have something challenging to work on. Day after day, month after month, and season after season, it was the same routine. I enjoyed my job—there was just no challenge in what I was doing and I wanted more. But that was all about to change.

We had been in our home about a year when a business bought an older retail building next door to us. The owner happened to be a member of our church, and I had wondered what the business was exactly, since the same cars were coming and going each day and nothing appeared to be sold out of the office.

One day, several months after they had moved in, Mike and I were hanging around after church and began talking back and forth with the owner. When there was a pause in the conversation, I asked, "Just exactly what do you guys do in that office next door to us?"

Tilting his head, he responded, "Why don't you come on over this week, and I'll show you around?"

Intrigued, I set an appointment with him for the next Tuesday morning.

As the time for my tour approached, I became exceedingly anxious, with almost a sense of excitement. Meeting a bunch of new people was scary, outside of my comfort zone, but I put on my best "brave" face and marched over to the office.

When I stepped inside, I noticed everyone busily working. Someone finally glanced up and asked if they could help me. I told her I had an appointment, and once she had verified it, she led me to the owner's office.

He gestured toward the seat, and we talked in general pleasantries for a few minutes before he asked, "So, did you bring your resume with you?"

Resume? What resume?

"Um… I thought you were going to give me a tour of your business and show me what you do," I stammered. "I didn't realize we were going to be doing an interview."

He chuckled, and then proceeded to explain that he understood I had done some bookkeeping and that he was looking for a bookkeeper. He revealed that they did geographic information systems (GIS) mapping, and asked, "So, are you interested in a job?"

"I am interested, but I know nothing about GIS, not to mention I already have a job." I disclosed that with tourism season ending, my hours would be cut to part-time during the following three months, and that if he was game, I would be happy to work for him part-time until March, and then we could re-evaluate me leaving my other job and going full-time. I didn't want to let a job go for one that may not work out.

He appreciated my discretion and agreed to my terms. And that was the beginning of a whole new adventure and many, many walks outside of my comfort zone and opportunities to grow.

While bookkeeping was the initial job, which included sorting and inputting several years of receipts into the accounting computer program, it did not end there. I began learning the mapping. I enjoy learning new things and, finding that I had a knack for this GIS skill, I continued asking questions.

I soon discovered different people have varying ways of doing the same thing. When I approached the two male supervisors about the discrepancies and inquired as to why we did not have a manual for consistency, it was as if I had accidentally set off an emotional firework display. You would have thought I was a woman questioning their "manly" authority. How dare I step out of line like that!

Their verbal lashing left me feeling like that stupid little girl from my past. It was near the end of the day when it happened, so I silently signed out of my computer, grabbed my keys, and slipped out the door. I breathed deeply the crisp clean air and, wiping away the tears, I entered my home and a space free from hatred and abuse.

A few days later, the first of these two supervisors approached me to say, "We have obtained a new contract, and since you are so enamored with having a manual, I think you would be the 'perfect person' to write this project instruction book." Smiling an evil smile, eyes glinting as his six-foot-three-inch frame towered over my desk, he dared me to take on the project.

Why the change of heart? I wondered to myself. *Thought I was incompetent!*

After working together for a few hours, learning the processes, and beginning the layout of the manual, the owner meandered by and inquired about our task. My supervisor quickly explained that he was writing a manual about the new project we had acquired. This satisfied the inquiry and the owner continued on his way.

Waiting for him to move past us, I questioned my supervisor directly, "I thought you wanted *me* to write this manual?"

"Oh," he chuckled. "Just ask my wife—I will have you write it and then I will take the credit for it." His glare dared me to question his authority.

We will see about that! My blood was boiling, but I managed to keep from spewing like a tea kettle on a hot stove. *We will see.*

Lunch soon rolled around, and this supervisor was off to devour something other than my self-esteem. I was unhappy with the way the manual was being formulated and had my own ideas of how it should read, so I went to the owner's office to discuss it with him. Showing him what had been drafted thus far, I shared with him my dislike for the direction it was taking.

"Is this your work or his?" he questioned, watching me closely to see how I would answer.

"His," I quickly answered and then continued, "I don't care for the way it is written. I would like your permission to change it."

Looking perplexed, he said, "I didn't think you were writing it?" There was a question in his tone.

"Yes, that is what he would like you to believe," I answered, choosing to spill the beans about the plan to take the credit for the work I was rightfully doing. "I was informed that I would be writing it, and he would be taking credit for it."

"Oh, he did now..." the boss trailed off curiously. "Well, I like your ideas. You just go ahead and write the manual."

I agreed to complete the writing and began the makeover. I had been working contentedly for an hour or more when I heard the owner's voice behind me, "How's it going?"

Moving aside in order for him to have a clear shot at my screen, I asked, "What do you think of the changes?"

"This is so much better than that other garbage," he praised. Then to my surprise he continued, "How would you like to be the lead on this project?"

Stunned but attempting to compose myself, I exclaimed, "I would love the opportunity!"

"Consider it yours," he said resolutely, patting me on the shoulder with a satisfied look on his face.

I wanted to jump up and down and shout, *YES! Yes, I absolutely want this!* Knowing that was not appropriate, I pasted an enormous smile on my face and said sincerely, "Thank you. Thank you for believing in me!"

"You deserve it," he said with a smile and walked away, leaving me in charge of the first of several multimillion-dollar projects and sending my confidence soaring to the moon.

As you can imagine, realizing their ploy to insult me was blowing up in their faces, the two supervisors momentarily backed away. However, the line had been drawn; and while I strived to work together as a team, the rift with the second supervisor quickly became a chasm as he set me up to fail on several occasions, only to find both the owner of the company and his partner supporting me.

While I was proving my strong work ethic and overall integrity, he was validating how unreliable and deceitful he was. My integrity placed me in the good graces of my bosses who defended me like a couple of papa bears and welcomed his resignation. Eventually, this man found his second job more enjoyable than dealing with me and walked away, leaving me in charge of the mapping and the other supervisor over programming. Soon after his departure, I earned the new title of executive assistant as well as a hefty raise.

The next year found our little company expanding rapidly. As executive assistant, I continued to have additional opportunities to spread my wings and soar as I took on the responsibility of hiring, firing, and training new employees. I kept an "open door" policy and counseled employees in a myriad of situations.

I was enjoying my newfound wings. Strengths and abilities I never knew I possessed rose to the surface. Over the next couple of years, the owners were traveling and out of the office much of the time; and I, too, traveled between the offices in Oklahoma City and Branson.

Ultimately, I convinced the contract owners and my boss to move the latest project exclusively to our Missouri office. Those that wanted to transfer had that option, but most had families in Oklahoma that were not willing to make the move. I interviewed and trained, along with my staff, dozens of people over the next two years, completing three projects and working on a fourth.

The jobs I worked on brought in money to help support the owner's new love—a software program that was going to "change the world." The only problem was the increasing amount of money required to pay the programmers to create the system.

As the price for my projects increased, the firm holding our contract informed me many times that we had to stop raising our prices, or they would be forced to give the contract to someone else. Passing this information along caused an increasing amount of stress between my boss and me. He was trying to complete his software program, and I was trying to keep more than fifty employees from losing their jobs.

It was during this stressful time that my boss was in a car accident. He had rolled his car on the tollway and was lucky to be alive. A few months later, he had to have heart bypass surgery. Whether it was the stress of his physical health or the downward spiral of his business, he became angry and mean.

Of course, I completely understood the emotional and physical toll of an accident, and felt terrible that he had to endure all of that suffering. And yet, being on the other side, I never knew when he was going to explode in a fit of anger or praise me for a job well done.

One day, out of the blue, he said, "Hey Lori, let's go have lunch."

I was hungry and agreed to join him. It started off nice enough; but in the middle of our lunch, he shocked me with an allegation—accusing me of stealing one of his computers. The entire restaurant could hear him yelling at me, and I wanted to crawl under the table and hide.

A knot formed in the pit of my stomach as my boss instantly became my dad.

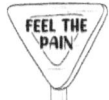

We had gone out for ice cream after my dad's step-daughter's graduation. He was already upset because she was going to a party with her friends instead of coming to celebrate with the "family." She lived with her father, so Dad had no say in what she did or did not do; and he hated not being in control.

Both of my boys, along with the rest of Dad's wife's family, headed for the ice cream parlor. I was in need of a bathroom and, upon asking the clerk, found it to be out of order. Before I could even respond, my dad was leaning over the counter yelling and screaming at her about city codes and ordinances. The poor kid was terrified and my attempts to calm the clerk and defuse the situation only fueled his rampage.

I was ready to leave and go home, but he demanded I place my order. I hated my dad for treating me and this poor clerk this way, and I hated myself even more for not standing up to him. I could not decide which was worse—the fact that I was allowing him to manipulate me in front of my children, or the further scene I would cause if I chose not to obey.

I smiled sweetly at the clerk as she handed me the small cone, apologizing to her with my eyes and whispering, "I'm so sorry."

Blinking away the memory, I glanced up to see my boss—a father-figure I had counted on and trusted for four years—staring at me. He had finished his tirade and was waiting for an explanation.

Through clenched teeth, I said, "I didn't steal your computer. It is sitting on the floor in the front offices."

"Oh," he responded sheepishly. Then, roostering up, he crowed, "Well, what's it doing there?"

Not bothering to answer his question, I pushed my chair back and stood as I continued, "The next time you decide to accuse me of stealing, you might want to have all the facts!" Grabbing my coat from off the chair, I marched resolutely out of the restaurant.

Unfortunately, that wasn't the end.

A few weeks later, I was rushing back to the office for the corporate meeting he insisted I attend, from a small project in a city about forty-five minutes away. I maneuvered through the downtown traffic until I was on the highway heading back to the office. Looking at the clock, I realized I would never make the meeting in time, but at least the project was finished, and I could work on my own agenda tomorrow.

Dialing my boss's number, I calculated what time I would make it back to the office. The ringing stopped and I heard his voice on the other end of the line and said, "I'm just leaving and will be about fifteen minutes late."

"That's fine," he responded.

Telling him I would see him soon and then hanging up the phone, I promptly made my way back to the office, pulling in and leaving the equipment in the car. I hurried through the front office door and looked past the front desk clerk and over to the conference center. No one was there.

"Where is everyone?" I asked, interrupting the clerk and one of the new owners.

The owner looked perplexed. "It was rescheduled. We had the meeting this morning."

"What?!?!" I am sure steam was erupting from my ears as my blood pressure shot through the roof. "Sure would have been nice if someone had told me!" I spat as I turned and stomped out the front door.

I busted my butt to get here! Why didn't he tell me when I was on the phone with him?

Grabbing a handful of equipment, I went back in and apologized to them both and said I knew that it was not their fault. It was his, and I planned to confront him about it the next time I saw him.

I was getting a second load from my car when he pulled into the parking lot a couple of spaces over. I was climbing in to grab the scanner when he loudly stated from the other side of his vehicle, "I suppose you are mad at me."

"Mad? No, I'm not mad! Incredibly frustrated, yes!" I retorted loud enough for him to hear me from inside my car. Deciding to back out of the back seat, I turned to face him at the exact moment he stepped around the back side of his SUV with a folding chair he had pulled from the vehicle.

"Well then, you just run this damn company if you think you can do a better job!" he screamed at the top of his lungs, while slinging the chair in my direction.

Un-flippin'-believable, I thought as I quickly moved to get out of the way. *You have got to be kidding me!* Fortunately, my body had regained most of its strength and enough flexibility to dodge the flying chair and watch it bounce across the ground as I stood there in disbelief.

The inner child in me leaped out, not caring who was watching or what the consequences might be.

"Listen!" I exploded, making a B-line toward the front door. I cornered him near the entrance and roared, "You are the one who asked ME if I was mad! YOU are the one who changed the meeting and didn't bother to tell me! And YOU are the one who threw the chair at me!"

Seeing that he was visibly shaking and trembling, my concern and love for him kicked in. I brought my voice down a notch and said, "If you don't calm down, you are going to have another heart attack!"

Our verbal confrontation ended as he walked through the door where I noticed that everyone had disappeared from the front office.

Great! Now I am going to have to apologize to my employees for making such a scene.

Though I felt justified in my actions, there was probably a better way to have handled it.

My mom's words rung through my head, *"If you'd just be quiet, Lori. If you would just shut up, none of this would have happened."*

Oh no. You are wrong, Mom! No one should have to take verbal or physical abuse from anyone, especially someone in authority!

My employees needed to understand that they could stand up for themselves, just as I had done, should this kind of incident happen to them.

Later that day, my boss quietly apologized to me in his office. There was no public apology, simply an, "I'm sorry, Lori. It's the medication I am on."

I could not believe what I was hearing, or not hearing.

That was it? That was all he had to say?

Borrowing a line from teenage Joshua, I thought, *Whatever!* and said, "Apology accepted. But don't you ever do that to me again."

Wow. As I walked back to my desk, I wondered at why I had found myself in this position again. *Blow up, throw things, yell and scream, punch or lash with a belt one minute. And because you have said, "I'm sorry," I am supposed to forgive and move forward as if nothing ever happened and we can live happily ever after. Just like my dad. That routine almost got me killed—in more ways than one.*

As I sat down at my desk, my mind traveled back to that dark time and place.

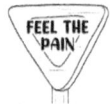

I was fifteen years old and tired of my life. I felt like an insignificant bug on the windshield of a passing semi. I had been beat up, spit out, and squashed flat with the windshield wipers now attempting to scrape my remains off with the swish, swish of the wiper blades.

Is life really worth living? I contemplated holding a bottle of pain pills tightly in my grip.

Yes, I had gone so far as to find a prescription, but did I have the courage to go through with it?

No one is going to tell me what I can and cannot do, I surmised, popping the lid open and dumping several pills into my palm. I was standing there in my darkened bedroom. I could hear Mom and Dad moving around upstairs, his loud voice demanding something. My little sister was asleep in her bedroom next to theirs.

How can she sleep through all of this? I wondered.

I stared again at the pills in my hand.

"But what if you don't die?" A voice from within resonated through my entire being.

Not die? What do you mean, not die? That is the whole purpose of taking them! I silently shouted back.

Now fear gripped my soul as I contemplated what might happen if the pills did not allow me to pass on to the next life. The repercussions, should my parents find me before it was too late, reverberated through my head.

I could see my mom frantically calling 911, the ambulance arriving, and being whisked off to the hospital as my dad sat sobbing to the police that he didn't understand why his little girl would do such a thing.

What exactly is in the next life? What if it isn't any better than here? If God really loved me, why would He allow me to have a father who is such a tyrant and a mother who cowers in his shadow, allowing her child to be subjected to such abuse?

Slowly the anger mounted, tenacity replacing fear, and I slammed the pills back into the bottle. There was a battle for good and evil going on inside my head and finally, when the dust settled, the good in me had won.

Why should I allow them to manipulate me, taking away my life and all I have to live for?

I was not sure at this point what I had to live for, but there was a determination in my mixed-up, teenage body and mind to survive this hell hole and to live to fight another day.

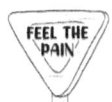

I chose the option of "live to fight another day" with my boss, too. Summer came and went, and we were experiencing the chain reaction of not heeding the warnings to stop increasing our biweekly billings for the mapping contract. I had tried for over a year to get management to stop raising our rates, to no avail. They refused to listen, and that fall, we lost the contract.

We laid people off weekly and, by the end of November, my boss had requested that I go from being his executive assistant, running several multimillion-dollar projects simultaneously and with an income that matched my abilities, back to doing the bookkeeping, mapping, and being one of the crew with an hourly first-year bookkeeper's wage.

I was not only insulted, but I had gained courage and self-esteem throughout my tenure there and chose to be bold in that moment. "I appreciate all you have taught me, and you have given me quite the education. However, I think your current bookkeeper, who has six kids, with one getting ready to go on a mission, deserves to keep her job. It is just Mike and me at home, and she needs this job way more than I do."

He looked surprised as I continued my proposal.

"I think you should lay me off instead. She will do a good job for you. Besides, I really don't think there is anything more for me to learn here." I was calm and collected, my voice unwavering.

Thinking about it for a few minutes, he finally broke the deafening silence. "Okay. Consider yourself notified that your last day will be December 17th."

"Thank you," I softly replied. A wave of relief washed over and through me. I had done it. I was leaving on good terms. With most of the employees laid off, we were down to a skeleton crew. December 17th could not come soon enough.

I had no idea that the pain from this accident was going to put me in a position where I had to face the emotional pain of my past at a deeper level. Suddenly, I was having to face a reality that there was more to heal than just my body, and that situation with my boss definitely helped me to tap into that.

Is there old pain—physical, emotional, spiritual, mental, or relational—that is coming up to be faced as you have been slowed down and are figuring out how to swerve around the obstacles you are facing?

Maybe you also have characters reminding you of days long past? Is there self-doubt, disappointment, anger, sadness, or hopelessness emerging? Most importantly, do you believe the painful struggles you are experiencing now are capable of catapulting you to higher ground?

"Our wounds are often the openings into the best and most beautiful part of us."

David Richo, PhD

Psychotherapist, Teacher, Author

Choice #4

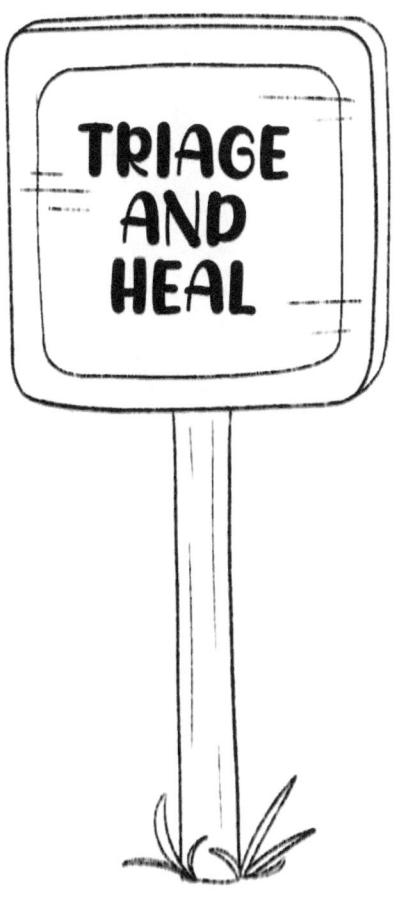

T he spring before I left my job at the mapping office, I had discovered a network company that sold text message marketing. It was an intriguing concept and way before its time. Because I enjoy technology and love to learn, this concept was fascinating to me; but even more than the technology, I found myself inspired by the leaders who hosted conferences, cultivated online communities, and used technology to issue challenges that took learning to an entirely different level.

Attending nearly every conference they offered, I found myself surrounded with positive attitudes and countless opportunities for growth—cultivating my self-esteem from a tiny seed into a healthy plant. Object lessons, vision boards, videos, and team meetings had me uncovering alternatives to how I looked and felt about myself and those around me.

These experiences helped me define an entirely different side of myself. In fact, I believe the new self-confidence emerging was what aided me on the battleground behind those office doors the last year in that business, in my personal life, and in my relationships in general. Tired of fighting and feeling that my entire life had been spent defending myself, I wanted something more and I sensed that I had the opportunity to experience a true transformation.

Using the tools and skills I learned, I set boundaries for what was acceptable behavior toward me and what I would and would not tolerate with family, co-workers, and friends. Once I learned that I no longer required anyone's validation of me to know whether I could accomplish a particular task or project, I commenced the process of releasing people whose only goal was to suck the life right out of me and consciously made the choice to surround myself with motivated, inspiring, and positive souls.

With all of this new awareness and energy, I realized that I was forty-eight and desperate for a change. While the good news was that my body was inching closer to pre-accident status, I was also facing some big life changes. Joshua was moving out of the house, work was collapsing around me due to the management's newly-warped sense of right and wrong and my desire to reach loftier heights, and I was feeling lonely and void of the ability to contribute anything of worth. There had to be something more for me to learn and accomplish, but what could I do?

As much as Mike was my biggest cheerleader when it came to putting the past behind me, he was not always happy about my traveling for work and these transformational events I had discovered. He tried to be as supportive as possible, but it was hard for him. Knowing there was a big change coming for me that was going to affect both of us, I knew I had to talk to him.

One evening after a particularly powerful seminar, I found Mike cleaning out the wood-burning stove in the living room.

"Honey, can we talk?" I asked softly as soon as I was standing near him.

Sweeping up the last of the ashes, he closed the door, stood up, and smiled as he turned to face me, affirming that it was a good time.

I wrapped my arms around him and started to pour my heart out, while staring deep into his dark brown eyes. "I know I am your wife, Chris and Joshua's mom, and an executive at the office. I know I am Mima to our granddaughters, a seminary teacher at church, and a boss to my employees. But..." I paused, momentarily averting my gaze to stare out the living room window.

We stood there silently for several minutes, simply holding each other. I could sense his anticipation at what I was going to say. He stood stiffly, not reacting, only listening. As the last rays of sunshine pierced the glass and danced across the living room floor, I found the words to describe my yearning and turned back to look him in the eyes again. "What I *really* want to know is: Who *is* Lori?"

The question hung in the air, a deafening silence permeating the house.

Standing quietly next to him, allowing him to take it all in, I watched for his reaction. I could almost see and hear the cogs and wheels rotating in his head, sensing that he was worried he might be witnessing a midlife crisis or, worse, the demise of our marriage. Mike was having his own challenges after being laid off with the crash of the housing market the previous year. While he managed to acquire odd jobs, completing home inspections and remodels, I knew he was fighting his own demons of self-worth around his ability to provide.

My employment paid well, and I knew we were fine, but it was Mike's manhood that was at stake. I knew I had to tread carefully.

"I want—no, I *need* to figure out who Lori is and what *she* wants to do with her life," I softly pleaded. "I want to step outside my circle of comfort and expand—figure out exactly what I am capable of accomplishing."

Mike's voice was barely audible as he whispered, "So, what did you have in mind?"

Good question, I mused. *I am learning tons about technology at my office and regularly bypassing the tech department and fixing the computer issues myself. I love technology. Maybe I would enjoy the creative side that programming offers. Chris seems to love it. He's become more and more proficient as a programmer and now leads a team and solves problems with code.*

"I think I would like to go back to school. I never really had the opportunity to attend a large college, and I would like to start with some basic classes and maybe work into a degree in computer programming."

There. I had said it.

I am committed, I decided while anticipating Mike's response.

His relief was palpable as the air rushed from his lungs, and he picked up the pompoms to cheer me on once again.

Mike was ecstatic about helping me to enroll, pick my classes, and even pay the tuition; and that fall, adding to my already busy load at work, I began my first semester at a university.

The first day of school, my nerves were working like a well-oiled machine, adding to the chill in the air. Throwing my backpack over my shoulder like a pro, I followed the entourage of students heading for the main campus and began my trek toward my first class wrapped in their youthful energy. Grateful that I had explored the campus the week prior to classes, and orchestrated the most efficient routes across the beautiful grass and tree strewn grounds, I maneuvered myself through the maze of buildings, bustling hallways, and the myriad of students traversing their own paths.

Feeling the burden of my book-laden bag, I proudly chuckled to myself. *This backpack could be pretty heavy by the end of the day. Good thing I've released the pounds of extra baggage, or I might have been doomed.*

Having lost over half of the nearly sixty pounds gained after my accident, I had reached a plateau that, despite consistent efforts throughout the past year, I still could not budge *until* I learned that by switching up my exercise routines to include different forms of exercise, my body would recalibrate.

At once, I added walking/running intervals, along with the elliptical and stretching I was already doing, giving my body the kick-start it was looking for. I also was blessed to have an incredible group of women who were eager to shed some pounds and inches along with me. We put together a healthy "plan of action," encouraging and holding each other accountable as we released our unwanted weight and celebrated each victory. This information, support, and strict eating regimen over the next several months helped me eventually regain my pre-accident weight status.

Metal chairs screeched across the floor as each student filtering into the Business Law class found a seat. Tentatively, I chose one near the middle of the room and close to the edge just in case I needed to make a quick escape. One hundred or more students chattered happily, greeting friends from previous classes or schools, or introducing themselves to new classmates. The air was filled with the anticipation of a new semester.

Wow, I'm really doing this. I wonder what is going to happen this year!

I enjoyed that class, along with English Writing, Psychology 101, a couple hours of study time, and the intermediate math classes that followed. Breathing a sigh of relief at completing my first day of school in nearly twenty-five years, I made my way back toward the parking lot for the fifty-minute drive home through rush hour traffic.

Squeezing all four subjects each into two days at school minimized my time away from the office and all of my responsibilities there, but it made for long days and even longer nights as I read, studied, and worked full-time at the office. My love for learning propelled me forward, and made it easy to excel in most of my classes—absolutely worth the extra effort.

Weeks went by and the crunching sound of fallen leaves could be heard among the other campus sounds. Like the squirrels skittering here and there gathering nuts, it seemed everyone was preparing for winter. Jackets came out of their closets and snow boots became the fashion. Thanksgiving came and went with its wonderful aromas, family togetherness, and the hustle and bustle of the upcoming Christmas season.

My final day at the office was rapidly approaching, and soon I would be out of a job. While I was elated at the thought of not working, I had also come to the realization that without my job, there was no money for tuition, the extra seminars, and other expenses.

Giving college my best effort, I ended the term with two A's, a B+, and a B. I was incredibly disappointed that I'd not achieved straight A's, belittling my efforts and wondering why I had not tried harder until my cheerleader reminded me of reality.

Being ever the realist, Mike pointed out that I had not only gone to school, carrying a full sixteen credit hours, but I had continued working forty to sixty hours a week at my office—managing an office full of employees and orchestrating the completion of three out of four multi-million-dollar projects well before their deadlines.

Mike is right, I concluded. *I've done well. I should be proud of myself for accomplishing all I did. Positive mental attitude, Lori! Look at what you made happen both at school and work—helping and encouraging other students and your employees. You are a strong leader,* I counseled myself. *Quit belittling yourself and start paying attention to all your successes!*

It had been a long week with finals and projects due for school and my last day of work for a company that had taught me so much and given me so many opportunities.

On December 17th, I hugged my boss goodbye and left the office for the last time, setting a small box of personal belongings on the front seat before heading home and into the next adventure.

What is next for me? I silently wondered as I pulled out of the parking lot.

When we got the news that Mike's dad and his wife would be coming for the holidays, we were happy. They had never been to our home in Branson and with all of the kids and grandkids planning to be present, it would be a wonderful celebration. More than anything else, I wanted my family to be together and feel my love and support for each of them.

One evening a few days before Christmas, we all bundled up and headed to Silver Dollar City for our traditional viewing of Dicken's A *Christmas Carol.* I loved walking through the city with its millions of twinkling Christmas lights. In the distance was the whistling sound of the Christmas train, carrying its passengers on another Christmas adventure. There was a chill in the crisp night air as we speedily walked through the street and down the snowy hill toward the opera house. We stopped briefly for warm drinks, and I smiled when the steam from my hot chocolate swirled up and around the enormous pile of whipped cream and up into the cool night air.

Once inside, waiting for the show to begin, I looked lovingly around at my small, innocent family, watching the excitement on our granddaughters' faces and listening to Mike and his dad banter back and forth. I was so grateful and took a moment to silently thank Heavenly Father for bringing us all together.

Thank you, Heavenly Father, for helping me to regain my strength. For inspiring me to have the courage and make the choice to fight for my physical and mental well-being and not succumb to others' visions of what I can or cannot do or be. For helping me defy the odds they gave me to work and continue to persevere, heal my body and my soul, and press onward toward my desired goal of being whole again.

There are no accidents, Father, and I thank You for bringing my family together at this time. For the opportunity to see my boys in their roles as fathers, and for bringing them safely through each of the struggles and challenges they have faced over the past several years. These are not my stories to tell, but hopefully someday, they will choose to share them and tell of how You loved them through such difficult times in such an infinite and eternal way. Thank You for helping me to understand that enabling only contributes to the problem, not the solution. For helping me to set boundaries and stick to them, even though it was the hardest thing for me to do. For helping me maintain open doors of communication even when it felt impossible. For strength to love unconditionally. For helping me to begin defining who I am. Please lead me along the path of discovery, continuing to open doors of opportunity for me to learn and grow. And lastly, Father, I want to thank You for bringing Mike and me together. I am so grateful he is not only my husband, but my best friend.

The holiday season would be yet another chance to apply my new mindset and boundary-setting skills. Lovingkindness was my goal. I was on a mission of sorts, not knowing how the changes would be accepted.

I turned toward the stage as the lights dimmed, snuggling into Mike's side and anticipating a wonderful evening. Come what may, I was making progress and becoming more of who my Heavenly Father desired me to be.

One morning shortly after the New Year had dawned, my phone rang. Recognizing the number, I enthusiastically picked up the phone and heard a familiar voice. It was the lead supervisor in Oklahoma on the project for which we had lost the contract.

I greeted her warmly, asking about the holidays and expressing how much I had missed visiting with her. We had built a real friendship that was not bound by contracts or project deadlines. I knew she was someone I could call for a reference or if I just wanted to talk, and I was elated that she was contacting me to check in.

We visited for some time and then realizing it was a work day for her, I teased, "I better let you go. You are at work and this is pleasure."

She stuttered and stammered, hummed and hawed for another minute or two.

What is this about? I wondered. This behavior was not normal for the woman I knew. If she had something to say, she just said it.

"What exactly did you call about, my friend?" I asked curiously.

She took a deep breath and finally shared what was on her mind. "Would you be interested in doing some consulting for us?"

I couldn't believe my ears! "Would I be interested? Heck yes, I would be interested! What exactly is it you want me to do?" I questioned.

She quickly gave me the details. The contract had been sold to a company overseas, and they needed someone to create a training manual for teaching the logistics to overseas employees, quality control work, and other tasks. There would be minimal traveling involved and the company would reimburse my expenses. It wasn't final yet, but she wanted to know if I was interested.

I couldn't think of a single reason not to be ecstatic.

"Thank you, Lori," she said. "You know more about this project than anyone else, including my own staff. You will be a huge asset. It may take a couple of months to pull it all together, but I will be in touch as soon as we have a plan."

I hung up the phone and did a happy dance before calling Mike to share the good news. Although I did not know when I would be starting my consulting business, I understood that this opportunity was no accident, and I was confident that it was the next step in my progression toward "the real me."

Attempting to stay busy until they got it all put together, I set about preparing for the project—meeting with an accountant and attorney and setting up my sub-s corporation.

With no school or job to yet tend to, I put additional effort into maintaining my health. I was forever working on my body, knowing that if I let my workouts slide, all the hard work I had accomplished incrementally over the last ten years could be lost in a flash. I continuously engaged in ways to build strength, along with the ability to move and stretch; and while I had met my weight goal, I now desired not only to maintain my efforts but excel.

Several months before my job had ended, my friend and colleague had encouraged me to start running. I had made some effort to run, adding to my repertoire of new challenges, even going with her to do some laps around the small track at our local gym. I was becoming stronger when the job ended; however, gym fees were again an unjustifiable added expense.

Because I was not stellar at running the hills around our home—especially during the icy months, for fear I would do irreparable harm—I reverted back to both speed walking on sunny days and exercising on my elliptical trainer as the alternative. I had completely worn out one machine since moving to Branson and I was working on killing off another.

I also relished the extra time with my granddaughters even more. Thursday was our special day, and I looked forward each week with anticipation, knowing we would romp and play, pretend to be princesses or scientists, tend to the garden, look for snakes and bugs, or enjoy a picnic and play in the park. Whatever we did, it was always an adventure.

I waited patiently for the consulting opportunity to come to pass, checking in with my friend every three or four weeks to see if a contract was forthcoming. The answer was always, "Not yet. They are working on the details."

There were a lot of pieces to put into place, and by the time April gave way to May, I finally had a contract and was enthusiastically heading to Texas to meet the crew that would be helping with this phase of the project.

Setting my own work schedule allowed me the flexibility to continue attending seminars. When they offered one in Chicago toward the end of July, I was ready and dove into more self-development. I enjoyed the event and jumped at the chance to join a coaching group for a nominal fee. I couldn't wait to pursue this avenue for learning, with another tribe of people and a totally new set of goals.

Engaging with this tribe consistently for thirty days was thrilling. I was expanding my circle of influence and beginning to understand the myriad of options available to help with my core objective—answering the question, "Who is Lori?"

Along with all the long hours spent consulting, I accepted the challenge and began decluttering both my life and my surroundings. It startled even me to notice how much I enjoyed the process, comradery, and positive changes I was making.

The final call was filled with successes, each of us sharing what we had learned and accomplished. When they offered an even larger challenge at the end of the call, I accepted and advanced to the next level.

This would be three months of exploration and weekly group coaching. I did well the first week and then fell behind and back into old patterns. I made excuses that I didn't have enough time and that there was too much going on, knowing full well that I was lying to myself.

Why am I falling behind? Why am I making excuses?

I was thoroughly frustrated with my less-than-stellar performance and shoved the opportunity on the back burner, attending only the weekly evening coaching calls.

If you can't do it right, I chastised myself, *then just don't do it at all!*

Listening to each coaching call, I heard how some had failed and others were rocketing forward, but both were discovering new layers to uncover and objections to overcome.

How could this be? Despite the fact that some have not completed the process with exactness, they are still coming away with huge wins, simply for putting forth effort?

This was a new concept and far from my "all or nothing" way of thinking.

On the final call of the month, the coach announced he would be giving each of us an opportunity for an extended challenge. Thinking, *I must be crazy,* I took down the information for the webinar to be held the final week of November. I loved the concepts he had been teaching and wanted a better understanding of how to switch my rigid thought process to a more productive approach.

But before I could attend the webinar, life took an unexpected turn.

Summoned by Mike's dad for a "corporate board meeting," we made our way to his home in Colorado and quickly discovered the reason for the gathering. His dad was getting older and thinking about retiring, and wanted to know if Mike was interested in taking on part of the business or if he should just sell the company.

Mike had talked for years about someday owning the storage business that he had helped his dad to build from the ground up. Every time his dad would holler for help with putting electricity in the new warehouse, adding fences and electronic gates, building a new wing, or making other improvements, Mike had always been "Johnny on the Spot," grabbing his tools and driving from Albuquerque, Branson, or other faraway towns where we lived.

It was a "no brainer" for us. Of course, we wanted to be a part of his dad's legacy. I was already working from home. Whether home was Missouri or Colorado did not matter. Over the next several weeks, we made arrangements to leave Branson and start preliminary packing.

Part of the arrangement would be to live in one of his dad's rental properties. He had tenants that were destroying the place and being evicted. It would be our responsibility to make sure they were out and repair or replace all damages before we moved in.

It was quite a job, and I was grateful that I was feeling so much better physically and emotionally.

One evening after a very long day of cleaning and preparing the duplex, I reminded Mike of the webinar I was going to attend that evening. I let him know it was a project I was fairly confident I would want to take on as part of my healing process, that I had no idea what the cost would be, but I imagined that it was probably going to be pretty expensive.

Mumbling something about taking a shower, he left me to my call.

Listening to the list of topics to be covered along with how the coaching process worked, I realized that this challenge would be like going back to school. If I wanted to transform my life, it was going to take commitment and effort on my part. I was all ready to sign up until that dreaded moment. The cost was announced and my mind spiraled.

This program is perfect! That's a ton of money! How can I make this work? Mike is going to mess his pants! He's not exactly a believer when it comes to this work.

Mike had *always* looked at the coaching I was attending in this light and could not see the usefulness of the process; but, I knew I was just beginning to experience the changes and that this program could catapult me into a whole new level of healing.

As this conversation swirled around in my head, Mike walked through the kitchen where I had set up home base and asked, "So, how much is it?"

Hesitating momentarily to gather my courage, I announced the amount.

Not missing a beat, he continued past me saying only, "That's a lot of do, re, me," and disappeared into another room.

I sat there feeling numb, then frustrated, and finally cynical.

I get it. It's a lot of money...

Then bringing to my mind all the things we had spent money on over the years, I created a mental list of all the *wasted* money that amounted to much more than what I was thinking of spending for a "good cause."

As he came back through the kitchen just a few minutes later, I asked him to just listen to what all the program entailed. He stopped dutifully and, without giving myself an additional moment to doubt, I began expounding on the many bullet points of positive opportunities this would allow me to experience. I included the facts that it was a three-year program with only a one-year commitment. After one year, I could decide not to finish if the process was unproductive. It would include assessments, goals, accountability, coaching, community, and more.

Maybe it was the enthusiasm in my voice or the persistent onslaught of program attributes, or maybe Mike was just exhausted. Whatever the reason, he noncommittally grunted and exited the room without any further conversation.

Hmmm. He didn't tell me I couldn't, I reasoned and immediately sent an email to customer service, explaining our move and expenses and asking if there was any way to make payments.

By the end of the week, we had completed our assignment in Colorado. The duplex was ready for our arrival in two weeks. When I committed to take the payments out of my business account, Mike begrudgingly agreed to let me join the program. I intended to get the most out of the opportunity, and I was anxiously looking forward to the kick-off webinar the week before Christmas.

Until then, I had plenty to keep me busy, including packing the house, celebrating our youngest grand-daughter's first birthday, and arriving back in Colorado to unpack so that Mike would be ready to start work by the tenth of December. What a whirlwind!

Lori, look at how far you've come! I acknowledged as I lifted a box and placed its contents on the shelf in the hall closet.

My gratitude was overflowing that my exercise regimen over the past ten years had brought me to the point where packing and moving across country was not the daunting, exhausting, earth-shattering process I had previously experienced. Capable of lifting and moving my own boxes, along with all the physical labor of getting the duplex livable was a confidence booster. I was able to acknowledge that all of my hard work to improve had paid off and was worth every bit of physical energy spent.

While engaging my muscles physically continued to be a process to enjoy each day, I was looking forward with childlike enthusiasm to the mental and emotional growth that I desperately desired to accomplish in the coming year.

I set physical, mental, and financial goals, outlining a picture for myself of what I was inspired to accomplish, focusing mainly on the physical goals the first few months.

The first goal I envisioned was crossing the finish line of my first big race.

My friend from Oklahoma kept encouraging me to run distance. I decided to "go big or go home." Time would not allow training for a full marathon; therefore, I chose the next best thing—I embarked on a quest to complete a half-marathon in Oklahoma City that April.

I knew she was familiar with the route and what it would take to accomplish. Showing her faith in me, she offered running tips and encouragement during my training and also a place to stay the weekend of the race. I could not pass up a deal like that!

What kind of distance should I start with? What pace should I attempt?

I researched running websites and talked to my friend and other runners I had met. I was determined to start with just a couple of miles and see what the outcome was.

Will I need a water bottle? Is the trail safe? What if I have to use the bathroom?

Again, taking tips from my mentor and other runners, I worked through the options.

Setting smaller goals for training and racing, I started running the nearby bike route. Early morning, running with the rising sun, quickly became my favorite time of the day. Jogging the short half-a-block to the bike trail gave me options for how far to go and how many hills I wanted to climb before work.

While finishing up my run one morning, I became determined, *My turtle pace is not fast, but I am consistent and able to run the distance without stopping.* I could feel the success expanding in my chest. *I'm so proud of you, Lori, for taking on this challenge! Keep up the good work,* I encouraged myself. With each week that passed, I added another mile to my run while maintaining my consistency.

Running at any speed gave me an unexplainable high. Listening to the birds sing as they woke, the river as it rushed past, and the "good morning's" of joggers and walkers out for their morning workout filled my soul in a way that no other exercise ever had.

Some days were definitely easier than others. At those times, I felt I could run like the wind and the distance was nothing. Other days, it took everything I had to keep going. I would convince myself that I could make it to the next tree, bend in the path, or to the top of the next hill. As I drew closer to the goal, I would set my sights on another target in the distance that became my new focus. Generally, these incremental wins would be enough to carry me through.

After a quick shower, I would usually head down the hall to my office for work. However, once each week, I attended the group webinar where we learned our weekly lesson, shared our wins, asked for help in particular areas, and received encouragement from our community while building life-long friendships with like-minded people.

Along with the webinars, there were weekly assignments to complete and group coaching calls to attend, challenges to compete in, and much to overcome. I was determined to complete it all, feeling blessed to have the opportunity and recognizing that with each passing week, I was overcoming, growing, and wading through the muck and the mud, tossing out the old way of thinking, and discovering a new, powerful, and tenacious ME.

Who is Lori? She is a warrior. Fierce and determined to fight for that person Heavenly Father created—to pull herself out of the mire of negativity others have heaped on top of her. It almost put her light out, but not anymore. She is committed to going the distance, overcoming whatever obstacle may pounce onto her path. She will succeed! Lori is a winner!

The weekend before my big race, I completed my first 10-mile run, making it my longest run yet, but falling far short, in my mind, from the 13.1 miles I'd have to run to cross that sought-after finish line goal.

Talking with my mentor and my community gave me the energy to move forward and do the best I could. I did not have a time in mind.

Simply finish. That is the goal.

Arriving at my mentor's home two days prior to the race, I was welcomed and immediately taken on a tour of the route. It helped to see the terrain, but it also increased the flurry of excitement building inside me. I had trained consistently, giving my all to every effort. Pushing away any and all demeaning thoughts that crossed my mind, I used self-talk and affirmations. I congratulated myself for my preparations and for showing up—painting mental pictures of myself as a strong, vibrant athlete.

The following day we picked up my race packet. Touring the expo with its multiplicity of wares was a fun adventure, and I came home with new socks, a running belt, and a t-shirt. From there, we embarked on a quiet afternoon walk in the park. My mentor gave me pointers on racing while we enjoyed the warm sun and gentle breeze. This beautiful, relaxing day was coming to a close as we pulled into the local Italian restaurant to eat an early fettuccini dinner before heading back to the house.

I wonder what tomorrow will be like, I pondered in her quiet guest bedroom as I prepared for the race. Checking each item off my mental to do list I recited, *Bib, racing gear, sports chews, water bottle, shoes, socks, ID. All I know is that I am going to have a wonderful experience.*

Knowing we would leave for the race at 5:15 a.m., I bid goodnight to all and went to my room. Saying my prayers and climbing into bed early in an effort to be well-rested was my grand plan. Unfortunately, sleep evaded me, and I began tossing and turning, dozing for a few moments here and there, only to wake up in a panic—thinking I had overslept and missed the starting gun.

At 4:30 a.m., my alarm rang out and I jumped up, heart racing as if I had already been running the race of my life. After dressing, I made my way to the kitchen to prepare my race morning breakfast of bagel and peanut butter. Wishing my stomach would be as quiet and peaceful as the house, I finished my breakfast, and then my mentor and I left for the adventure of my life.

After parking the car, we made our way through the fading darkness and crisp morning air toward the corrals where the runners would gather. I could hear the muffled sounds of the loud speaker and music as people moved in every direction like mice scampering about. Energy and excitement ignited the air, creating a pull—like a magnet sucking me in. Drawing closer to the starting line, we found ourselves surrounded by hordes of participants, onlookers, and security. I was thrilled to be among so many athletes, as the butterflies in my stomach proved.

Let me run as fast as they fly, I prayed.

The excitement of the crowd was invigorating, and I nearly leapt over the barrier to claim my spot behind the pace runner holding his time high for all to see. Although it was still cool, I knew it would not take long to lose interest in my jacket. I peeled it off, handing it over to my mentor as I began alternating between jumping up and down and stretching my muscles to warm up and prepare for takeoff.

The music was blaring, and everyone began dancing and chattering with each other. The girl next to me had run the marathon before, and we talked briefly. Then came the moment of silence and the countdown began.

Cheers exploded all around me as the gun went off and the entourage of runners pressed forward for their turn to cross the starting line.

Oh my goodness! Never in my wildest dreams could I have imagined this scene. I became lost in the moment, forgetting my timidity and unleashing the warrior within. I began dancing and singing, uninhibited by the expectations of others, as we inched forward along with several thousand others, finally reaching the starting line.

The onlookers were loud and encouraging as I ran across the rubber timing mats and into my first big race, alongside firefighters and military persons running in full gear and people running in memory of lost loved ones. This energy propelled me forward.

I can do this! surged through my mind as we rounded the first corner.

Unable to contain my exuberance, I pulled out my cell phone, attempting to capture the crowd, the excitement, and the moment, snapping several pictures while running toward the first incline.

Thousands of people were running this race, each one with a goal and reason of their own to accomplish. The first couple of miles, I felt as though I was running on a cloud and nothing could stop me.

At mile seven, I told myself, *You've got this! You are going to reach your goal!*

Though the onlookers and cheering crowd began dwindling in number as the miles ticked by, those that remained were still amazingly supportive.

Then we split and the marathon runners went one way and half-marathoners ran another. By mile ten, fatigue was settling in, and the muscles in my legs felt like limp noodles. I found it hard to stand up straight. Taking each breath was an effort. Dehydrated, I searched the street for the next water station.

Just a few more blocks, I coached myself. *Keep your head up.* I continued, finding the next small goal to obtain that would get me closer to the finish line.

You can't let them win, Lori! You have to complete the race and prove to everyone that they were wrong about you!

Doubt kept trying to creep in, telling me I would not have the energy to continue.

NO! I silently screamed. *I can do hard things!*

I looked around for my mentor, hoping to see her encouraging face, but everything became a blur of colors and lines as I remembered the day that had made this one possible—the day I had looked Mike straight in the eyes and declared, "This is not acceptable" and set out on this journey to prove that they were wrong.

They said there was nothing physically wrong, so there was nothing I could do, except take pain meds and antidepressants; but I didn't give in and kept searching for answers. They said I wouldn't be able to work part-time, and now I am running my own full-time consulting business. They said I wouldn't be able to lift more than ten pounds repetitively, and I just finished renovating a home, packing up all our belongings, and moving across the country. They said I wouldn't be able to do normal, daily activities, and now I am running a half marathon. I've shown them now, haven't I? I thought as the colors and lines cleared, becoming people in colorful jackets and clothes. With new focus and renewed courage. I determined to reach the finish line. The crowd was gradually growing in numbers, and one person was shouting, "You're almost there!"

Several turns came and went and still no sign of a mile marker.

I should go back and slap the person who said I was almost there. I know they were just trying to encourage, but I am so exhausted and just want to know where the finish line really is.

Finally, mile marker twelve came into view. My head was spinning, and my legs were so tired I could barely lift them off the ground. Muscles twitched and screamed from the beating I was putting them through. My knees were swollen and growing larger with each passing mile. I felt as though I was going to stumble and fall at any moment, as picking up each foot became a huge effort.

If I could just see my friends, I was nearly crying. *I know that would help me to push past this fear.* But I could not find them. Just when I thought I would have to stop, the crowd began growing larger and the encouragement began to hit my ears and soothe my soul.

"Half a mile," someone yelled. I trudged through another turn and into downtown, watching the pavement as I shuffled along, attempting to keep my mind focused and moving forward.

"Almost there! You can see the finish line," another bystander announced.

I looked up and sure enough, there was the banner waving high above the finish line—drawing me in and begging me to complete my goal.

I can see it!

Confidence surged through me and flooded my body with renewed energy and strength. Pounding the pavement determinedly, I drew ever closer to the prized finish line.

Again, I searched the crowds for my mentor. Three more blocks. Two. One. And there in front of me was the finish! I threw my hands in the air and screamed, "WOO HOO! OH YEAH! I DID IT!" as I crossed over the finish line and into a new realm of winners, completing my race in 2:30.26.

I did not care that my legs were burning with fatigue and beginning to cramp or that my bladder was ready to rupture, for something far greater was happening as my heart rapidly pounded. Sheer delight overcame me. Tears of joy, accomplishment, and pride rolled down my face as they placed my finisher's medal around my neck. Words cannot describe the flood of feelings and emotions washing over me.

I did it! I did everything they said I could not do!

Oh the pride that filled my soul at accomplishing this goal. My heart nearly burst.

"I did it! I really DID it!" I exclaimed the moment I saw my mentor.

Every fiber of my body ached. I had pushed myself to incredible heights. I had won the battle the doctors said I could not win.

"Take that!" I wanted to yell and scream at them. *"You know nothing about me and what I can or cannot do! I am Lori Giesey, and I can accomplish anything I set my mind to do!"*

Finding my breath, I reflected briefly, tracing the steps I had just completed. As I mentally crossed that finish line again, my immediate thoughts surprised me:

What's next, Lori? If you can do this, what will your next goal be? Maybe I'll finish school, or learn to play the piano, or maybe I'll...

You can see how important all my cheerleaders, my mentors, and my regimen were to my triage and healing process. Even when I was mostly done with the doctors for my physical well-being, I was clear that it was time to work more deeply on my insides—to find the real Lori and heal all the stuff that was keeping her from living an amazing, joyful life.

Have you made the choice to triage and heal? What steps are you taking to heal old wounds? Who do you have in your corner—supporting, listening, and cheerleading—when the road is long and hard?

What are you saying to those who try to pull you down or force their limitations on you, including that voice in your head that can be so cruel? What kind of communication skills or tools would you like to gain in order to make this easier?

Can you see yourself as an emerging warrior? Will you choose to let her rise?

"Keep moving ahead because action creates momentum, which in turn creates unanticipated opportunities."

Nick Vujicic

Motivational Speaker

Choice #5

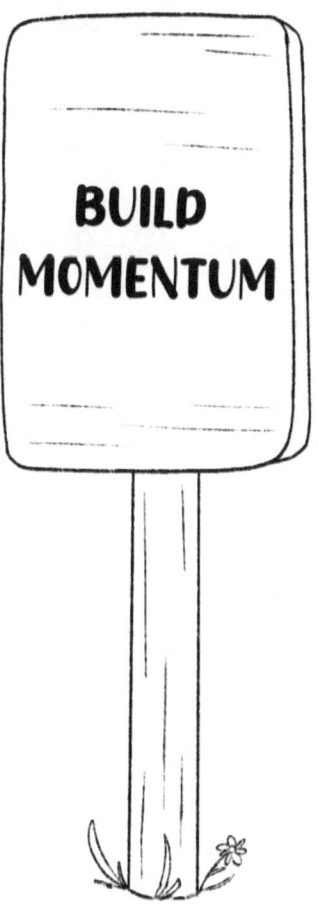

I continued pounding the pavement almost daily, setting new distance and time goals in an effort to clear the clutter from my subconscious, expand my beliefs, and stretch to reach my true potential.

At a party just a few weeks after my race, a friend inquired if I would like to participate in a relay race. Each runner on the twelve-person team would take three rotating turns, together running a segment of the nearly 200 miles of road and trail to reach a designated destination. I was elated to be invited.

My excitement and momentum escalated over the next several weeks as I trained for the event. I had never competed in anything like this, so everything about it was new. We did not have any team meetings or training, so my friend and I encouraged each other and prepared the best we could.

The day of the event, we found our van included the two of us and four men who were great at making us feel welcomed and part of the team. We arrived and checked in that evening as it would be a 5:00 a.m. start for the team.

Our van was the first of two for our team, with the first six runners in our vehicle. As runner five, my first leg was over six miles up to and across a dam, and along the side of the large mountain lake. The late morning sun glistened off the water, creating a marvelous view to enjoy. I ran well throughout the evening, including picking up an additional three and a half miles for one of the men in our van who had become injured during his initial run.

I finished my third and final leg in the heat of the following day. Our van had satisfied our portion of the mileage, and we could now kick back and wait for the rest of the team to finish. While not the fastest runner on this team, I was pleased with the twenty-plus miles I had run and, though exhausted, was feeling quite accomplished. I had learned again that I could do hard things and that I wanted to help others build their champion spirit. In fact, I decided to captain my own team the following year, and build more momentum for myself by helping others realize their greater potential, too.

Fall was now upon us, and I worked out for the remainder of the year at a local gym with a personal trainer, building strength and tightening my core during the winter, so I would be ready to run again come spring. Having dedicated so much of the year to running, competing, and proving I could overcome my physical challenges, I wanted to take the last quarter to tackle my other goals of decluttering my environment, creating an inspiring and peaceful home, spending more time with Mike, and strengthening my relationship with God.

I ended the first year of my quest to "find Lori" feeling appreciative of all I was learning about myself. Checking my goal list for the year, I came to the conclusion that many aspirations I had written down would be a continuous process of peeling off layers and diving deeper into the original goal.

Grateful for the momentum I had created over the past twelve months, I used that energy to propel me into the future as I set my goals for the coming year. Focusing on the first quarter, I wrote down specific goals I wanted to accomplish and was a bit surprised as the thought "write a book" came to mind. It was true that as I had decluttered, soul searched, and worked to strengthen my relationship with God, I had thought much about writing down my story; but I had concluded that this was part of our family history, and I was not ready to work on this aspect of our genealogy. Heavenly Father, however, had different plans and made sure I was assigned to an extraordinarily insightful coach.

On the initial call, he set the pace by asking me, "How do you want me to coach you?"

Momentarily taken aback, I processed the question and confidently replied, "Call it like you see it!" I then explained that I wanted him to be honest with me. When he saw that I was not putting forth my best efforts, I wanted him to call me out.

I knew that if I truly desired to find myself and become the best of what Heavenly Father sees, I would have to put forth my whole self—not just the positive, safe side. I would also have to face the parts of me that I saw as atrocious, scary, and hideous that needed to be uncovered, exposed for what they really were, and disposed of.

This is not the time for me to crawl safely back into my proverbial shell.

The stage was set for me to shift my thoughts, choose to break out of that confining space, and take those first steps into the light. Exposing my innermost thoughts and feelings, I would be able to see other possibilities and allocate room for growing, expanding, and creating a new and more empowered me.

With questions still pending on exactly how to move forward, I determined to squelch the seemingly endless nagging to complete this project that, with each passing day, weighed more heavily on my heart and mind.

Sharing this goal of writing a book with my coach brought it into the open, exposing plausibility. However, with each goal I set to work on the manuscript, there seemed to be a piece of the old self clawing, grabbing, and pulling me backwards—instilling doubt and fear while belittling me: *"You are not an author!"*

I had worked so hard to uproot these thoughts and yet here they were again. Scoffing, the voice would continue, "You do not have the competency to tackle a project of this magnitude! Who do you think you are? You are so pitifully stupid."

This was not the first time I'd heard this voice.

After the three of us had finished our meal, I cleared the table full of dinner dishes and began filling the sink with warm, soapy water. Christopher was just a toddler, and I could hear him playing contently nearby. The evening might have been peaceful if not for the noise of the television in the next room.

Stupid TV.

I hated the constant noise that man insisted on listening to.

How can he possibly study with all that—

My thoughts were interrupted by a loud crashing noise, followed by a deafening stillness. Intuitively, I knew exactly what had happened.

Christopher had watched both of the adults in his life rotate the television from one side of the sofa table to the other at least a hundred times. I am sure he thought he was a "big boy" and could help by moving it back to where it belonged.

Instantly, waves of panic enveloped me and I ran, dropping the dish cloth midstride. Racing around the corner, I scooped my son up in one sweeping motion, clutched him firmly to my body, and tore past where he sat on the couch doing his homework, looking temporarily stunned by the sound of the television smashing into the ground.

I shot past him like a bullet being fired out of a gun, terror flooding my veins at what he might do. As soon as my feet hit the cold bathroom floor, I slammed and locked the first door behind me, and reached for the second door to our bedroom. Christopher was crying, not understanding what was going on.

With the second entrance locked, I slid down the wall, holding tightly to my precious cargo. I rocked back and forth as he beat on the locked door, screaming a slur of profanities that would make a sailor blush. And then he said it: "You good-for-nothing, worthless piece of shit! Open this door NOW!"

That was the last time a man ever spoke to me like that. And yet now, after all these years, here I am—doing this to myself? What's up with that? Where is this voice coming from? Mike would NEVER dream of talking to me this way.

This coach was good. He helped me navigate my subconscious's crusade to keep me safe and small, which felt more like a crusade to destroy me as it used only the information it had— decades of abusive language, perceived failures, and self-doubt—every moment I took the tiniest step toward my goal.

"Look at you! You've been working on this for months and haven't written a single chapter! You are so lame!"

The perfectionist in me took over, and became more and more dismayed at my failure. The old voices in my head demanded residency in the new space I had created for my writing, leaving me doubting my ability to complete my objective. I could not see that although my writing was unfinished, there was so much more to accomplish before I could complete my mission.

I spent countless hours looking in the mirror, using self-talk and affirmations—steadfastly ridding myself of old limiting beliefs and guilt, creating positive new pathways for my thoughts to travel, and leveraging new mental strategies to bring myself up to the next level.

Along with the coaching experiences, I had moved forward with the goal of putting my own team together for the relay race in August. I held team meetings, day and night training runs, and shared what I had learned from my previous experience about packing light, food choices, and the fun we would have so that my team members would feel more confident in themselves and could enjoy the journey.

I experienced several moments of clarity during this training, recognizing that this was the kind of work I wanted to do—helping others realize their God-given potential and not hide behind the excuses and negative voices of others, past or present. I became caught up in recruiting several new athletes and had been working on various aspects of my character for several weeks, again leaving the book floating aimlessly in Neverland, far from my thoughts and aspirations.

I began cleaning out the clutter in earnest, tossing or donating things I'd held onto for decades, always afraid I might "need" the item someday. Fear was my old nemesis—the one so many had used against me, keeping me squelched and under their thumbs.

Knowing these old thought processes would keep me from my potential, I relentlessly replaced my feelings of anxiety and fear with words like *strength, power, boundaries,* and *winner.*

Learning to walk away from toxic relationships was hard as I built a barrier of protection around myself, especially with family. The first time I set a boundary with my father despite the feelings of fear consuming me, I took my first step into this new world.

Dashing into the kitchen to get my phone before the last ring, I glanced at the screen to see who was calling. Recognizing the number, I took a deep breath. *What will I be chastised for this time?* Hands trembling as I contemplated not answering, I finally decided to not prolong the inevitable.

I put on my happy voice and answered, "Hey, Dad. What's up?"

We talked in generalities for a few minutes before he started whining about how much he missed the kids and grandkids and how no one ever called or went to see him. It was always the same dreaded conversation—griping and complaining, but never taking action to change the pattern.

"Well, Dad," I began, not wanting to explain all the reasons why people avoided him and his self-righteous behaviors, but hopeful about sharing a viable solution. "Do you still have that computer camera we gave you for Christmas several years ago?"

"Probably. Somewhere..." He proceeded to complain about having to find it.

Hesitantly, I spoke up and volunteered, "If you will find the camera, I'll help you set it up so you can Skype with the kids."

Suddenly, his tone switched from whining to condescending and loud—his oldest tactic for reminding me that he was in charge. "I don't want to use a camera. You know they are watching us and listening in through those cameras and—"

I boldly interrupted his nonsensical jabbering, "Well, Dad, if you have nothing to hide, what difference does it really make?"

He did not appreciate my rebuttal and raised his voice another set of decibels, proceeding to explain how naïve I was to not know that even my smart phone is another tool for them to watch my every move.

Rolling my eyes and taking a deep breath to soothe my increasing anxiety, I calmly said, "Dad, we are just going to have to agree to disagree on this subject."

He barked back in an attempt to continue the conversation, again raising his voice, nearly yelling at me through the phone.

My entire body trembled as I broke in sternly, "Dad, I would love to visit with you if you would like to pick a different topic of conversation."

He started in again, and again I said, "Dad, you have a choice: we can either agree to disagree on this subject and pick a new topic, or if you want to continue this conversation, I will hang up and talk to you again another day. Either way is fine with me. It is completely up to you. In fact..." Attempting to help him change the subject, I inquired as to how things were going with his wife's health.

We managed to stay on this new topic for only a moment or two before he again returned to the previous dialogue.

I repeated the available options, "Dad, I am going to agree to disagree with you, and if you would like to continue talking today, we will have to find a new topic. Otherwise, I will hang up and talk to you another time..." Again, I changed the subject matter.

When on the third time he went back to the original topic of conversation, I simply but firmly declared, "I love you, Dad, and I will talk to you later. Goodbye!"

This conversation left me feeling empowered and alive. No longer was I that little girl left holding the sacks full of guilt and the disparaging words of others.

As each opportunity presented itself, I bravely marched away from those determined to set their expectations and destructive beliefs upon my shoulders. I set new boundaries, allowing those with the baggage to carry it themselves. This momentum added to my courage and confidence that I could stand on my own platform and make the decision to surround myself with like-minded individuals without someone else's approval.

When race day finally arrived, we gathered at the house to decorate the two vans and, after saying a prayer, began our adventure. I had no idea that this was going to be such an amazing journey, which would launch me onto a completely different path than I ever imagined taking.

For this relay, I would be runner number twelve— the very last of my team to compete in each of the three legs. I wanted to have the experience of bringing my team across the finish line but had not considered the fatigue I would experience from being up all night and the one responsible for getting our van to the exchanges on time. This left me very little down time, but I was determined to complete our objective.

My first two races were tough, but nothing I could not handle; however, running the final segment was a completely different experience. By the time I began the climb to the first ridge, I had been up for more than thirty hours, either running or navigating the majority of that time.

My turn had come in the warmest part of the day; and although there were trees of all shapes and sizes, their branches gave little shade from the intense rays of sun and beads of sweat soon sopped through my headband and down my face.

I turned on the tunes to keep my motivation flowing as I navigated the rocky terrain.

Climbing higher and higher toward that first 9,000-foot peak, it soon became apparent that running was becoming less of an option. I'd struggled through several weeks of Achilles tendon issues and was not feeling one hundred percent healed. My breathing became more labored as I sucked in the thin mountain air. With every step, my legs were rebelling as muscles tightened, clenched, cramped, and screamed for me to end this perpetual beating.

Each team was allotted a certain number of hours to complete the race and time was swiftly running out. In an effort to finish the last eight and a half miles as quickly as possible, I resolved to speed-walk the uphill and run the down.

The forest of trees began thinning out and the grass next to the trail's edge became taller as I wound ever higher. I maneuvered as fast as my weakening legs would carry me, keeping my eyes on the dirt trail to prevent catching my feet on any random rock jutting up out of the ground. With each turn of the trail, I thought,

This has to be the top, only to round the bend and find yet another series of inclines looming.

Discouragement was setting in and though speedily traversing the trail by hiking standards, my pace was incredibly slow. The chattering of the squirrels and chirping of the birds mixed with the turmoil of self-doubt and disbelief bubbling to the forefront of my thoughts.

Fear was clawing at my psyche, screaming that I was a failure. Shoving back the negativity, I began playing "mind games" to create a distraction, congratulating myself for continuing and using my newly acquired self-coaching skills to build momentum and propel me forward with positive thoughts and determination. Dreading the moment my body refused to take that next step, I urged myself onward and upward repeating, *"Pick 'em up... put 'em down... pick 'em up... put 'em down!"*

At last, I reached the edge of the first ridge crossing. The view of the valley from the top was breathtaking. The majesty of the hills with the palette of colors from the grass, trees, and wildflowers created an exquisite view. Wanting to take it all in but reminding myself of the moments scurrying by, I began winding my way back down the other side, running the downhill, as I had committed, to keep from falling further behind.

Reaching the end of the trail, I found the paved street where the water station stood between the two trailheads. Seeing that I was exhausted, the volunteer came bustling across the road to meet me, removing the bottle from my hand and replacing it with a cup of cool water to drink. I paced circles around the station while he replenished the liquid in my bottle and my teammates cheered me on.

I took it all in.

"You can do this, Lori!"

"Half-way there!"

His task complete, the Good Samaritan handed off the full water bottle as their shouts of encouragement continued.

"You've got this, Lori!"

"We will meet you near the finish!"

"Good luck!"

Energized by the water and the encouragement, I headed up the trail for the next ridge, the reassuring shouts from the team fading as I began the next phase of my climb.

Rounding the first corner in the trail, I became aware of the silence that suddenly surrounded me. No longer was there music coming through my headphones. I fidgeted with the armband for nearly a minute before successfully removing my phone. Bringing the phone up with the next pump of the arms revealed nothing but a solid black screen.

Realizing I was wasting precious energy I did not have to spare, I screamed out loud and raised my head to the cloudless blue sky, "FINE! YOU WIN!!"

Then just in case someone happened to be nearby on that godforsaken mountain, I continued the conversation in my head, *If I can't listen to music, then let's have a "come to Jesus meeting"!*

Adding to the perspiration, tears began streaming a path down my cheeks as I poured out my heart to my Heavenly Father. Screaming and crying, praying and listening, I trudged along the trail. We conversed about finding myself and how that played into what Heavenly Father's plans were.

Suddenly, I imagined myself writing my story.

Should I be telling my story to others?

For many years, I'd told pieces of my car accident journey when I had felt it could help someone with a particular struggle or trial they were experiencing. And inevitably, at some point during every one of these conversations, I would hear, "You should write a book and tell your story."

Poo-pooing their comments with a wave of my hand, I always brushed the idea off with a, "Yeah, maybe someday," never intending to do more than perhaps write the story in some form for my posterity.

I thought my story was just that—mine. Who else would care what I had been through or what crisis I had overcome? I could not fathom that sharing *my* story would make a significant difference to anyone and had relocated the idea to the far recesses of my thoughts, wanting nothing to distract me from my focus on my progression as a healthy woman, a strong wife, a loving mother, and a powerful business owner.

But on that mountain, I felt God was answering my questions of "Who am I? And what is my purpose?" in a very personal way and showing me that my story was the key.

Expressing my doubts to His ever-listening ear, I began, *God, I am not a writer. How can I possibly do what You are asking of me? I don't even know where to begin! I mean, thank You for showing me more of my potential, but I am going to need You to help me believe in this new vision of me.*

On that mountain, I experienced the most rewarding talk with God. I pulled strength from the new self Heavenly Father and I were creating, and dragged my butt up the remainder of that mountain as swiftly as my depleted, aching body could.

The switchbacks coming down the ridge were steep and near the mountain's edge, where one slip of the foot would send me rolling down, head over heels, to the rocks below. Purposefully stepping as far away from the ledge as possible, I reached the end of the trail and climbed the final paved incline, arriving at the village center.

My eyes began scouring the groups of shoppers and cheering onlookers, searching for my team as I ran the final mile.

Where could they be? Why are they not here? Dismay momentarily took over my better judgment. *They are supposed to run in with me!*

Reaching the end of the shopping plaza, pavement turned again into a dirt path leading across a grassy hill. Nearing the gondola, I saw my team waiting and welcoming me. What a sight they were to behold!

I did it, I inwardly cheered. *I am almost there!*

I was a winner, and I was not going to let anyone or anything take that from me. Completing the course was the objective, and all that remained were a few twists and turns down the final descent. My team trailed behind, allowing me to lead them in for the victory so we could cross the finish line together.

As the team ran through the finish line and came to a stop, emotion engulfed me. I could barely breathe through the gushing tears as the enormity of what my team and I had just accomplished surged through my entire being. The words raced assuredly through my mind confirming yet again:

I can do hard things!

My talk with God on that mountain had lit a fire within me. He was nudging me in a direction far outside my comfort zone. I was scared to death, but knowing that I had to step out in faith and try, I covenanted to embark on this journey with the Almighty. I had no clue how or where to begin. I only knew it was part of His plan and my purpose for being here, and that somehow God would help me find the way.

Throughout the rest of the year, I made concerted efforts to understand the writing process. I talked with a wonderful woman who graciously took time to walk me through the route she had taken to publish a book.

I set about figuring out chapters, putting together an outline and, by the end of the year, was completely discouraged and ready to throw in the towel. Using the holidays as an excuse, I put my notebook aside and conveniently forgot all about writing while I took on additional challenges that a year or two before would have brought me to my knees. Running was a godsend, and I thrived on any new adventure—even flying to California to participate in an obstacle course challenge with ten others from our coaching team.

We climbed walls twice our height, ran through tires, sloshed through mud and muck on our bellies, and even climbed a warped wall. The pinnacle for me was tackling the obstacle that had terrified me the most.

For weeks, I had been visualizing myself swinging from ring to ring above the muddy abyss with strength and power, gripping the steel circles with confidence. First one and then another, maneuvering successfully to the other side.

When my turn came, several of the team members had already made their attempt at crossing, quickly dropping noisily into the muddy water below. Grabbing the wet ring, I felt my hand slip immediately, so I leapt back to my starting position, reached down, grabbed a handful of dirt, and rubbed the dry soil between my hands.

Jumping again for the circle swaying well above my head, I grabbed hold and held on for dear life. My body swung like a pendulum, arms reaching forward, and with strength and determination, I used momentum to propel me onward. Stretching out and grasping the next ring and the next just as I had envisioned it, I reached the middle where most had fallen.

One of my teammates shouted, "Look at Lori! She's going to make it!"

Hearing my name and the cheering of teammates gave me even more courage and confidence, until I eventually found that last ring and swung safely to the other side with a giant smile spreading from ear to ear.

I felt giddy with girlish excitement and pride at conquering my fear and learning a new technique in the process. I had not given up at the first sign of failure, but instead made a split-second choice and stepped back, regrouped, and created the momentum to take me through to the finish.

Soon, I was surrounded by teammates patting me on the back and congratulating me.

Oh yeah! Watch out world—here I come! I chanted to myself while laughing and joking with the others.

We ran on to the next obstacle, and soon we were at the finish line. Grabbing hold of each other's hands, we slid down the slide, screaming as we plunged into the muddy water below.

Leaving California, I was adding another notch to my belt of accomplishments, having built wonderful relationships, connected with my magnificent coach and team members in person, and acquired additional knowledge to strengthen and fortify my resolve. I couldn't wait to apply the tool of visualization to my other goals.

As winter blew in with its cold and snow, I found myself reflecting back on my second year in the program. I could see where I was working diligently, chipping away at layer after layer of the negativity and abuse that had previously trapped my spirit and held me down. I was proud of my efforts and celebrated each accomplishment with childlike zeal and enthusiasm.

Preparing to step into my third and final year of the program, I took a good, long look at the new Lori emerging and taking shape—a force to be reckoned with—and established my next goals to encourage and strengthen my transformation.

Physical goals were easy to write down. I wanted to reach new speeds and distances, adding core and strengthening back into my routine to mold my body into a well-tuned running machine.

Financial goals were a bit tougher for me as I had discovered that I was allowing fear of money or the lack of money to control me, instead of me controlling money. These were memes from my childhood, and I desired to rid myself of them.

Last were the goals that would make my life even more enjoyable. This is where I found my attention reverting back to my big commitment to God. Having recently experienced multiple opportunities to tell and retell my story to others, I had felt the presence of God gently encouraging me repeatedly, with ever-increasing pressure, to move forward and complete my commitment. Completing this task would definitely bring joy to my soul.

The snow melted away, and as the days grew longer, I found myself outside running the trails near our home. Passing others on the trail, I began wondering about their stories. Who were they and what had placed them on this path?

On one such excursion, a young man with a small boy and girl at his side came into view. The kids were laughing and playing, tossing rocks into the river, and then racing around their father. As they moved in my direction, I waved and said, "Hi," as was my custom while running on the trail.

As they waved back, I noticed his limp. Glancing down, seeing his metal prosthetic leg, my mind filled with questions.

Was he in an accident? Had he been hurt serving our country?

He seemed so happy to be spending time with the children, even though life had dealt him this challenge.

What tales could he tell?

The prodding began with renewed urgency and vigor to take up my pen and begin anew. Over the next few days and weeks, impressions would pop unexpectedly into my thoughts, causing me constant reflection on the pledge I had made with God several months prior and His gentle nudges for nearly two years.

At times I wanted to bark back, "I tried! It didn't work! I don't know how to do this!" However, faith had taught me that anything is possible with God's help, and I anguished over how to bring about a finished project.

I had left "writing a book" as one of my long-term goals, but my coach and I were busy pursuing other objectives and had not spoken about writing in months. And to be perfectly honest, at this point, I had never even told Mike that I was thinking about publishing a book, let alone the specifics of my promise made to God on that mountain.

The venture was weighing heavily on my mind one evening, and I awoke several times throughout the night, knowing I had been dreaming but not remembering about what. Only a gnawing in the pit of my stomach and thoughts of blank pages filled my mind.

The day dawned bright, and I took off early for a run before my chiropractic appointment. Feeling incredible about my ability to run and planning my next racing adventure, I could not wait to share my progress with my doctor.

I enjoyed his positive outlook on life and the support he gave me to go and do more than most people my age, encouraging me with each new challenge I presented. He was fun to banter with, and we often found our conversations leading into wonderful gospel topics.

This particular morning unfolded as usual—until it didn't.

He was chatting away as he adjusted my left side and then walked behind me as I rolled onto my back and waited for him to come around to the right. Suddenly, the chattering ceased, and the room became deadly quiet. I could sense that he had literally stopped midstride on his way around the table.

I paused for a moment, concern escalating in my mind.

"Are you okay?" I questioned, craning my neck in an attempt to see him.

Silence pierced the room until I heard his slow and careful steps moving forward into my line of sight.

Turning toward me, his eyes locking onto mine, he unequivocally announced, "You are supposed to write a book."

Tears instantaneously burst from my eyes, rolling down my cheek and onto the table. Looking up at him, gulping between sobs, I knowingly asked, "How did you know? I haven't told anyone—not even Mike."

Softening his gaze, he quietly responded, "The Lord told me to tell you: You need to write a book." His smile told me that he somehow knew that this was not the first time the Lord had spoken to me about this, and I was facing a very clear choice to listen or ignore it.

Head spinning in disbelief, I left the office and went straight home. For whatever reason, the Lord was giving me a second witness, cluing me in to His higher purpose. I could not ignore His calling any longer.

With a new resolve and energy, knowing the Lord was on my side, that I was on His errand, I scrounged around for the notes I had written so many months before. Opening a new document, I began typing.

"Chapter One."

In our next coaching session, I told my mastermind about my heavenly experience in the doctor's office. Astounded at the power of God pushing me into action, the team rallied, supporting and encouraging me to "get 'er done!" My coach agreed to hold me accountable to the deadlines I set.

I made an agreement that upon completion of that first chapter, I would send the draft to two trusted friends. The first was the lady I had turned to initially to learn the writing process. Ending up on the same coaching team that second year, we had become fast friends. The other was my wonderful accountability partner, who was making great strides toward her own goals.

It wasn't easy to relive the journey as I formed each sentence. I typed, erased, and revised, as my story brought old emotions and limiting beliefs to the surface. Eventually, the old stuff slowed my process as I worked through each upheaval. Making some deadlines and missing others, I finally finished that first chapter.

Holding my breath and hitting the "send" button, I launched the file into cyber space.

There it goes, I exhaled, wondering what kind of response I would receive. Within a few hours, I had my first reply and then the second, both full of encouragement and overflowing with praise at how this piece had come together.

"Thank You, Heavenly Father!" I exclaimed, reading again the flattering words and positive reinforcement. Floating on cloud nine, I prepared the next set of goals. And on it went—writing, reworking, struggling, and overcoming.

Squeezing in chunks of time, an hour here and two hours there, between my consulting business, church calling, and training, I finished the second chapter and was knee-deep into the third when our mentor announced he was bringing a guest to the next call.

"Her name is Amanda Johnson. She has a team that helps people through the process of writing and publishing. Amanda is the transformational author of the book *Upside-Down Mommy,* an Amazon #1 Best Seller," he announced proudly. "She will be joining us to answer..."

His voice trailing off as a plethora of questions began forming in my mind.

What does the process of editing and publishing the document look like? How about the cost and dates for completion? What happens if you miss a deadline?

Inquiring minds wanted to know, and I was ready to receive answers.

When the day finally came and Amanda was introduced, I listened intently to what she said and could feel her positive energy and intention to help others succeed. She talked about her book and the struggles she faced as she brought it to print.

By the end of the call, I felt a connection and an enthusiasm for another answer to prayer. Understanding that Amanda was the person to help me get there, I reached out to her over email.

Reading and rereading the email before I sent it, I thanked her for being on the call and for reviewing my manuscript. I explained that it was not yet complete, but sent her all I had.

"Looking forward to hearing from you," were the words I typed as I thought, *I am opening myself wide up here!* Noticing the fear attempting to move in, I decisively hit "send" before I could change my mind.

No turning back now, I decided, falling to my knees and pouring out my heart to my Father in heaven. *I'm putting my trust in Thee. I know this is no coincidence Amanda has come onto the scene at this time. I am but the scribe. If this is to move forward, YOU have to show me the way.*

There was no place for fear in this process. With each test of my fortitude threatening to dismantle my very being, knocking me down, dragging me to the edge of the mental and emotional cliff, attempting to hold me back from accomplishing my goal, I refused to give it any power over me.

Clawing my way back, affirming my ability to not only win each battle, but become the conquering force, I made every choice to dig deep inside my soul and fearlessly tackled each new challenge just as I had done during the darkest days of my childhood. I now knew that God was on my side and that with Him at the helm, I would not fail.

Moving forward with faith, Heavenly Father has provided encouragement from Amanda, my coach, and friends, and continues opening doors I never dreamed were possible.

I believe that I have always had the courage to dig deep and rise up as a conqueror. I used this strength as a child in the struggles to protect my mom and fight for truth and justice. Later as a teenager, I built on this momentum as I chose to live. And now this has accumulated and propelled me to complete the writing of this book.

I cannot help but wonder: *Just where will this momentum take me next?*

Once you start gaining some momentum in your healing and goal-achieving process, the sky is the limit. For me, the physical training helped to accelerate my journey, and achieving those distance and event goals increased my self-confidence. I absolutely needed that momentum in order to start making real progress on a project like a book, which felt way too big and heavy. I needed that momentum to make good on my choice to listen to the promptings.

Where have you built momentum in your life? What steps or progress have you already made? What choices and actions have helped you to build confidence in yourself and your capacity to heal and grow? How are you using that momentum to propel you forward?

Conclusion

THERE ARE NO ACCIDENTS

This journey started with an accident—or was it?

Writing this book and reflecting back on all that has transpired since that eventful day more than seventeen years ago—when my car and I were launched into the air and tumbled to the ground—I cannot help but wonder about the voice I heard before the accident: *"Slow down" and "You cannot hit this lady!"*

And the inner voice guiding me not to fill the many prescriptions the doctors gave me and to fight for real answers—the one that heard the functional capacity evaluation findings and yelled, "This is NOT acceptable!"

And the many voices of those with whom I shared my story, who told me to write down my journey.

And the utterances from deep inside, inspiring me to expect more of myself and to do *"whatever it takes"* to move forward.

And the innate understanding that giving up is *not* an option.

And the bold mindset, cultivated through tragic experiences in my childhood and young adulthood, that screamed, *"You cannot hurt me!"* and fought at all costs for truth and justice.

And the heavenly messages, through blessings with hands laid upon my head, encouraging me to continue along the path.

And my "come to Jesus meeting" with my Heavenly Father up there on that mountain.

And the nudges I felt, and the directive from God through my chiropractor emphatically telling me, "You need to write a book!"

And the promptings to figure out who I am that led me to finding a community and pursuing deeper healing. Peeling off layer after layer. Expanding my capabilities. Getting knocked down only to pick myself up, brush myself off, and try again.

All of these—an accident?

I think not!

Choosing to turn right onto that back country road that sunny December afternoon was a single, solitary decision amongst millions of other choices that I have been making throughout my life.

Some would say it was a mistake—an accident.

And you know? Right after the accident, I would have agreed with them. The effects of that decision were painful, scary, and paralyzing in so many ways.

But these many years later, I'm not sure I can subscribe to the idea that any of this was an accident.

Of course, I don't believe that our Heavenly Father wants or plots our pain, but this journey has taught me that His ways are higher than mine.

Who would I be today, if I hadn't taken that road that day?

Who would I be if I hadn't been forced to look inside and dig deep for emotional courage and physical strength I did not know I had?

Who would I be today if I had not applied myself to improving my health and mind every day?

Who would I be if I had not made the decision to go looking for Lori?

My experience of crossing that first half-marathon finish line would definitely not have been the same, or may have never even happened, had the doctors not tried to tell me I "should not... could not... would not ever again..."

Refusing to conform to others' beliefs, and choosing for myself what I am capable of, has made all the difference in my life.

And I have come to one conclusion: *There are no accidents.*

My Heavenly Father knew what was ahead of me that sunny day, and He's been here right beside me ever since—shouting at me to slow down, inspiring me to swerve around and fight the doctors' nonsense, nudging me to feel the pain but continue pushing past my limits, guiding me to triage and heal with the help of friends and mentors, holding me and creating momentum in my life throughout this writing process, and inspiring my next vision.

If not for that right turn, I'm not sure I would be inspired to gather teams of people to help them realize they're stronger than they think they are. To come together, in safe environments, to conquer and overcome challenges and to know that they can do hard things.

I am not sure I would be writing a children's series to empower our precious little ones to learn that life is hard but that we have the right and the privilege to choose its direction with our next step. That when things happen unexpectedly, like my car accident, we can choose to play the victim and blame others or we can be brave, lean in, embrace the moment, and conquer the challenge we are facing.

Yeah, that settles it.

There are no accidents.

Only choices.

Whatever your heartache and experiences may be, there is one thing I know:

YOU are a child of God, and He knows you intimately because He created you, and He has an eternal plan just for you.

Only you get to determine whether you will let others tell you who you are, and what you are going to do and be, or whether you will choose to stand up, brush yourself off, and take hold of your life—your destiny—and become all that our Father in heaven intends for you to be.

The journey begins with your next choice.

Will you choose to immerse yourself in the guilt, shame, and pain of your perceived reality? Or will you decide to take action and determine that what is in the past is no longer relevant?

Today, you can choose to empower yourself and reach for exalted heights.

Life is about choices.

I had no idea it was really just the beginning.

THE FINISH LINE

Wrapping up that three-year self-improvement program in December of 2013, I felt I had traversed quite a large portion of the trail, discovering many an answer to the question of "Who is Lori?"

Slowing down when the way became steep and showing myself grace when I needed to take a moment to rest along the path. Swerving around all the obstacles that could have distracted, detoured, and thwarted my growth. Feeling the pain, but also the freedom, of letting go of relationships that no longer served me and healing the wounds from the traumas of my past that had been exposed. I had come a long way, but I didn't have any inclination how much further I would have to travel and the momentum that would propel me forward as I wrote the first edition of this book.

I spent a good portion of 2014 - 2015 focusing on both my writing and running. The running came much easier for me and gave me a way to support others. Training together and sharing what I had learned, I ran races to support others on their first athletic adventures as well as several half marathons of my own. The writing, however, did not come as easily. There were so many stories and deep wounds to heal, and neurological pathways to reconstruct, and I had barely scratched the surface of the writing process.

In 2015, Mike and I purchased a home of our own, and I wrapped up my consulting business.

Life was good, and I took the last few months of that year and into 2016 to "just be," enjoying more freedom to run and hike while deciding what I wanted to do next. I also began working with the young women at church and, as always, enjoyed being in their company.

Then in July of that year, Mike's dad was diagnosed with cancer and our lives were immediately consumed with doctor appointments, hospital stays, and hanging on to each other as we rode this emotional roller coaster.

While I continued working on the book and supporting Mike and his dad, I was asked if I would take on the position of Relief Society President of our local ward, a women's organization in our church. It was here that I felt I could really put the things I had learned into practical application, helping families and nurturing women with everything from family welfare issues, teaching gospel lessons, and even offering practical classes like clutter-clearing. I enjoyed spending time with these women, listening to their stories, and helping each of them to feel seen and heard.

Then, in October of 2017, Mike's dad made his journey to the other side. This loss sent a great rockslide tumbling down upon our family, giving us one more opportunity to reinforce the knowledge that we can do hard things. Moving the emotional debris off our path, we officially took over the mini storage business operations Mike and his dad had built together and run for over thirty-eight years.

Of course, this presented a new set of challenges.

By 2018, with our little town growing into a bigger city, storage complexes were popping up all over, and I realized I would have to drag Mike and the business out of 1979. It was hard for him to change colors and logo, build an online presence, and step into the twenty-first century because it meant changing everything he and his dad had created together. However, the future success of the business depended on it.

I continued to use running and hiking adventures as my therapy and loved escaping off on a trail to reground myself and put life back into perspective, but most of the time, I found myself on these trails alone and craved the companionship of others to enjoy these moments with me.

In January of 2019, I found a group of runners who met at the local high school track early on Wednesday mornings. I was thrilled at the prospect of having fellow athletes on the adventure with me.

My first day, I awoke early to make sure I was ready and dressed in several layers to combat the freezing temperatures outside. I was filled with anticipation as I grabbed my additional outer gear and headed for the park, as the track was covered in snow that had fallen throughout the night.

Snowflakes continued falling out of the cloud covered sky as we gathered at the corner, under the lamp post. After introductions and a group selfie, we set off on our run, crunching through the snow and enjoying the quiet of the morning while most people, even on a warm day, were still sound asleep in bed.

We talked as we jogged and laughed at our craziness. I mean who goes running at 4:30 in the morning, especially with several inches of snow already on the ground and large white flakes continuing to float from the sky? Crazy... yes, but also magical.

Throughout the winter months, we continued to meet and run the track.

One morning, as we headed out on our group warmup mile, one of the guys mentioned that several of the runners were going to Huntsville, Utah, in September to run a marathon and asked if I was interested in joining them.

I was thrilled at the prospect. Having trained once before for a marathon, I'd missed out due to injury and spent the past two years wondering if a marathon was ever going to be in my future. (Note: I wrote out about that injury and its impact in my chapter of *You Can't Make This St*ry Up: What If It's All Happening for Us?*)

As he talked, my hope increased.

If not now, when?

I decided if I was ever going to run one, this was the time. I had a team of marathon runners, several who had qualified and run previous Boston marathons, and others who were training to hopefully qualify at this race. I knew they would all be willing to share their knowledge with me on training, nutrition, and more.

What do I have to lose? I thought as I looked at the website and registration details.

I shared the race information with Mike, and he gave me his blessing and encouraged me to embark on this adventure. I was filled with joy at the possibility of this event actually coming to pass.

September 21, 2019, was race day and still seven months in the future. There was a lot to learn and a training program to figure out. I spent many a track day going over ideas, asking questions, and trying different nutrition in order to figure out what worked best for me.

By the middle of May, I had my training dialed in and spent the next eighteen weeks working my plan. I usually ran early in the morning, before anyone was up, so as not to interrupt the family, business, church obligations, and all of the work to self-publish my book. Plus, Mike was still deep in grief. It was a lot!

Each week was intense and pushed me to my next edge. I struggled with lack of sleep, intense training, and the stress of life and often questioned my ability to add another element every week. I swerved around these obstacles and continued giving myself smaller, incremental goals like running to the next mailbox or finishing the lap before the song playing through my headphones ended. Anything to keep me going just a little bit further.

This all paid off. With each new week, I used the momentum gained to complete the next level of training. As race day approached, I was pleased with myself and what I had accomplished. I was feeling stronger than I had ever felt, and my pace was the fastest I had ever consistently run. I was elated at how far I had come in such a short amount of time.

By the time race week came around, we were more than ready to go. The five of us women who were staying together took off toward Huntsville Thursday morning, chatting and singing along to our favorite running tunes, discussing great books, and enjoying other conversations on the seven-hour drive.

The anticipation was palpable as we arrived at our destination. Quickly, we unloaded our luggage, then piled back into the car, and headed off to drive the route we would be running when the starting gun went off on Saturday morning.

The fall colors were vibrant oranges, yellows, and reds, and we commented on how beautiful the course was going to be. A river meandered along portions of the course, the sunlight winking off the water as we drove by.

While the driver navigated the course, I recorded a video I would watch several times over the next thirty-six hours. It helped me to see and begin to prepare in my mind for the up and down hill portions, where the water stations would be found, and the beginning of each new mile. I used bedtime to visualize myself running each mile and overcoming any challenges or obstacles that portion of the race might toss my way.

It was nice to have an extra day to relax, and we spent it checking out the race wares at the packet pick-up center, grabbing a couple of extra nutrition packets, and enjoying the jovial atmosphere. We decided to jog a couple of miles that afternoon just to get the jitters out, found a restaurant for dinner, and then headed back to the condo to prepare for the next day.

As I laid out my clothes, shoes, bib, and other running gear, I reflected back on my training. I knew

I had done everything possible to prepare and now it was time.

I struggled with sleep as the thoughts of the doctors and the functional capacity evaluation flitted across my mind. Finally, I drifted off just before eleven and slept until my alarm woke me.

Today's the day. I opened my eyes, rolled out from under the warm covers, and stepped onto the carpeted floor. Quickly, I put on my race garb and headed downstairs for breakfast. We each had our own routines, and the nervous energy was thick in the air as we each gobbled up our food and headed for the car.

Snow had softly fallen the previous night, and the air was chilly. The buses were going to start up the canyon at 5:30 am, and as crisp as the air was in town, it would be even colder once we arrived at the start line closer to the top of the mountain.

Music helped us all lighten up a bit on the short ride over to the bus pick-up, near the finish line, and we piled onto the bus with renewed energy.

"Mind if I sit here?" I asked one of the runners from our group.

"Not at all," she said and slid over a bit.

The drive up the mountain took about twenty minutes. I sat in silence thinking, *What have I gotten myself into?* A deep sigh emanated from my body. *Twenty-six miles,* I pondered, another sigh escaping. *The furthest I have run is seventeen and a half...*

Several sighs later, my friend next to me who had run this race before and was hoping to qualify for

Boston gently asked, "Do you mind if I give you a piece of advice?"

"Not at all! I would love some advice because I am kind of wondering what I have gotten myself into."

There was a deep knowing in her eyes. "Focus on the current mile. Don't think about what you've already done and don't worry about what is still ahead. Just focus on the current mile."

Instantly, a wave of relief swept over me and my breathing regulated.

"Thank you." A tear rolled down my cheek. "Thank you!"

Reaching over, she gently squeezed my hand. "You've got this," she encouraged as the bus rolled past the start line to the white tents and long row of porta-potties.

Single file, we exited the bus and headed past the source of the blaring music and into the large tents to stay warm. We had about forty minutes until the start of the race, and I didn't want to be cold.

The man with the megaphone counted down every five minutes. As the time ticked by, the butterflies began twisting and turning. I gathered all the extra clothes I had on and placed them into the race bag. Venturing out into the cool morning, I was captivated with the snow that was glimmering on the trees as the sun began to rise.

I took a couple of selfies, dropped off my bag, and made one last trip to the facilities. Coming out of the bathroom, I could hear the voice on the loud speaker encouraging people to line up. I slipped into line and began jumping up down to keep my muscles warmed up as the cool morning air hit my bare legs. Taking a moment, I snapped a few pictures of myself at the start line. I wanted to capture every moment!

Before I knew it, the countdown had begun. Three... two... one! Bang! And the starting gun announced the start of the race.

"Focus on the current mile" was exactly what I did. Clicking off the first mile, I thought to myself, *Holy cow! You are actually doing this, Lori! You are running a marathon! Look at you go!*

By the time I reached mile three, the sun was fully up and glistening off the snowy treetops. Beauty was all around me and runners encouraged each other as we moved along, passing some and being passed by others.

At four miles, I took in some nutrition. Next came miles five, six, seven... I continued to focus on the current mile and was feeling exceptionally great. By the time I reached the halfway point, I had officially run my fastest half-marathon race.

Surprised at the paces I was clicking off, I was beaming in disbelief that I was still feeling so good at mile sixteen.

Around mile eighteen, I began to tire and focused on my friend's words, repeating them over and over in my mind.

Focus on the current mile... Focus on the current mile...

As I ticked off mile twenty, I began to feel some cramping. Having never run twenty miles before, I figured it was just normal fatigue. At mile twenty-two, I stopped to use the porta potties, take in some extra nutrition, refill my water bottle, and tie my shoes. Back out on the course, the cramping ensued, and I began intervals of walking after several minutes of running to ease the pain.

My pace became slower and slower as the pain increased. By mile twenty-four, my walking intervals had increased in length, slowing my pace even further.

By the twenty-fifth mile, I was half-running and half-walking but I kept pushing forward. Then, halfway through mile twenty-five, I was limping. The pain was so intense. Feeling defeated, I pushed those feelings aside.

I am so close, and I am going to finish!

As I completed mile twenty-six and rounded the corner, I could see the finish line banner and all the people cheering the runners. Over the music, I heard the voice of the announcer calling off the bib numbers as the racers came across the finish mat.

I wanted so badly to finish on a high note. My time was not what it could have been, but that did not matter. All I wanted to do was run across the finish line, so I decided to kick it into gear.

The pain surging through my body was excruciating, and turned the last stretch into something of an old black and white movie playing out in slow motion. The noise ceased and everything became still and silent. The crowd seemed to know I was in terrific pain, and I could see the silent crowd gasp and put their hands to their mouths in shock. Unable to run, I limped forward, refusing to give up.

Someone from the crowd cheered, "Keep going! You're almost there!"

Tears began to form in my eyes and then, one hundred feet in front of the finish line, it happened...

Time stood still as my left leg gave way and I was propelled toward the ground.

What just happened? I panicked, trying to figure out why I was suddenly sprawled out on the pavement.

I heard someone asking in a faraway voice, "Are you okay?" Two people were standing by my side, but I was lost in my own darkness, not processing that all the noise and activity was all focused on me.

Chaos was coming from the sidelines as someone was yelling, "That's my mom! That's my mom!" My mind swimming in an adrenalin euphoria, I was unable to process that it was Chris vehemently trying to get past security and the barriers to get to me.

The two runners at my side urgently asked again, "Hey... are you okay?"

Shaking my head to clear the crazy fog, I responded, "I... I think so," and raised myself up with my arms into a push up position and attempted to stand by placing my right leg underneath me.

Each of them grabbed an arm to help me to my feet as Chris arrived on the scene. He was there when I tried to put my left foot down on the ground and as I began to teeter to the side, he caught me and wrapped my arm around his neck, letting the two runners know he could take it from there.

Things were so unclear, I did not realize it was Chris who was at my side.

I was focused on the sudden awareness that here I was… approximately one hundred feet from the finish line… and yet… I was unable to advance toward it. Thoughts began spinning and swirling around in my head.

Lori, how can you run over twenty-six miles and not be able to finish? How am I going to complete these last one hundred feet? What the heck?

Suddenly the race coordinator appeared from the other side and out of the corner of my eye, I saw her wave her hands, signaling for a wheelchair.

Hell NO! I screamed in my head and then heard myself cry out determinedly, as a single tear escaped and rolled down my cheek, "NO! Don't make me sit in that wheelchair! PLEASE! I want to finish my race." Additional tears joined the original one as I pleaded again, "PLEASE, just let me finish my race!"

Still unaware that it was Chris at my side, I was coherent enough to know that I was not willing to stand passively by and have others tell me what I was or was not going to do. I didn't care who they were. I had gone down that road before. I didn't like the way that turned out and I wasn't going to do it that way again. I was taking control of this situation, whether everyone liked it or not. This was *my* race, and we were going to do it MY WAY!

Seeing the determination on my face and understanding she was not going to change my mind, the coordinator rolled her eyes at me as if to say, "And just how do you propose to do that?"

My mind had finally started to clear, and I realized Chris was by my side. Relief enveloped me like a warm blanket, and he seemed to read my determination to finish at all cost. He gripped my hand hanging around his neck and prepared to help balance me as the two of us moved forward together.

I had taken one or two hops forward when the race coordinator saw that I was going to use Chris to steady myself and hop my way to the finish line. She moved toward me and brusquely grabbed my other arm and wrapped it around her neck, telling the driver of the wheelchair to follow close behind.

Yes, I'm finishing.

Leaning on these two like a pair of crutches, I stepped forward with my good leg making my way toward and across the finish line, using my own power.

Slowing Down and Embracing the Moment

"Will you sit in the wheelchair now?" The coordinator's voice was gruff as I leaned forward, allowing the volunteer to place my finisher medal around my neck.

Smiling brightly at the volunteer, I gave her a wink and plopped my broken body into the chair. "Yes! I'm happy to sit."

Chris walked protectively beside me as they wheeled me across the grass and over to the first aide tent where he helped a medic maneuver me from wheelchair to the makeshift lawn chair gurney before texting his dad to let him know I had been injured.

I thought maybe I had dislocated my hip because I literally felt it slip out of the socket, but as the medic moved my leg around and attempted to relocate it, I screamed out in pain. Excruciating pain. Pain like I had never felt before, EVER! He immediately stopped and addressed his companion. "Call the hospital. We will need to take her by ambulance."

As they shuffled off to make the arrangements, I looked up into Chris's worried face.

"I've never heard anyone scream like that, Mom" he mumbled.

"I'm sorry, but I've never felt pain like that before." I smiled to let him know I was okay. "It was like a lightning bolt shot right through me."

He stared back at me, brows furrowed and a concerned scowl crossing his lips. But as I lay there contemplating all that was transpiring, I had such a sense of peace. Reaching for his hand, I looked into his big blue eyes filled with apprehension.

"I don't know what is going to happen, but I do know that I am determined to embrace this moment... come what may!"

I had learned my lesson the hard way before when I'd allowed anger and frustration to take hold, which wasted valuable energy resources and delayed my healing process.

I'm not letting that happen again!

I had finished my race and that was a huge accomplishment, even if it was not the way I intended.

When the ambulance arrived, I made light of what was going on and even took a picture inside the ambulance with one of the medics while I held up my medal for all to see.

"For when I look back on this experience." I smiled brightly as I snapped the photo. Even though I was experiencing pain, I knew my attitude would determine my outcome.

It was a short ride to Ogden Medical Center where they quickly wheeled my gurney into a room and transferred me onto a hospital bed. The EMT's disappeared as the ER nurse promptly took my vitals and questioned me about my injury.

"I'll bet the doctor will want some x-rays," she stated confidently before abruptly turning around and walking out the door.

Watching the minutes tick away, I had plenty of time to process what had happened as I waited for the ER doctor. When he finally arrived, his lousy attitude and bedside manner struck me first. It was like he had a chip on his shoulder, and I was the cause of it.

When he asked what happened, I gave him a rundown of the details. He appeared to be put off that I had injured myself running a race, like I had deserved what had happened. Each word of explanation seemed to irritate him more.

Jerk. Just like all the other doctors who made me feel alone and judged when they should've been helping me!

He barked that he was going to order Xrays and stomped out as quickly as he had come in, leaving me feeling personally attacked and my joyous spirit deflated.

Stay positive, Lori. Maybe he's having a rough day, I coached myself.

Not long after the Xray team departed, the door opened, and I cringed, thinking it was probably Dr. Charming (sarcasm intended).

"How are you doing, Mom? Have they figured out what's wrong?"

I was so happy to see Chris's face and began telling him about the ER doctor's wonderful bedside manner and how he nearly had me in tears.

"I'm not sure if it's just racing fatigue or this injury, but I'm a hot mess!" I said mustering a chuckle as I tried to lighten the mood. "I hate it when people, especially doctors, upset me so easily."

Chris stood guard by my bedside, texting his dad between conversations, trying to catch him up on what was unfolding while we continued to wait.

Although Chris was keeping me occupied in conversation, the adrenalin rush was subsiding and I was becoming antsy. My heart did a flip-flop when I saw the door begin to open. Then I giggled as Heidi, Chris's girlfriend, and her ten-year-old son peeked hesitantly around the corner, making sure they had the right room before stepping in.

"Come on in," I encouraged. "Join the party!"

With some friendly faces in the room, I knew I wasn't going to have to face that pompous ass of a doctor alone, and my courage felt revitalized and ready.

Come what may.

We all chuckled as Heidi commented sarcastically, "Great place for a party!"

I was so proud of Heidi. She had run her first half-marathon that morning, and I was anxious to hear about her experience. Enthusiastically, I enquired, "How was your race? Tell me all about it!"

As she shared the details, it occurred to me, that if she had not chosen this particular race for her half-marathon debut, Chris most likely would not have been at the finish line when I needed him.

Wow! You just never know. A wave of gratitude swept over me, and I sent up a silent prayer. *Thank You, Heavenly Father, for placing us all here together today.*

While Heidi was wrapping up her story, we were startled by Dr Charming when he dramatically threw open the door and strode noisily over to my hospital bed, glared down at me, and announced bluntly, "You've broken your hip, and you'll need a hip replacement."

I'm sure my jaw dropped to my chest as a million questions flew through my mind.

I have just run an entire twenty-six-mile race, and the diagnosis is that I need a hip replacement? You've got to be mistaken!

I was having a difficult time articulating anything but eventually managed to eke out, "Will I ever run again?"

"Hmph..." he scoffed loudly as he headed toward the door, barely exited the room, and then stormed back in.

"Here!" He shoved a phone in my face with a picture of my Xray pulled up. "See this? You fractured the head of your femur, and now *we* will have to replace it."

Still in shock, I repeated myself, "But... will I be able to run again?"

Glaring at me through clenched teeth, he snapped, "You're going to have to learn to walk again, first!"

And poof! He was gone.

Emotions rolled through me. I was so devastated, angry, hurt, and wanted to tear him apart limb by limb. Glancing at Chris, I could see he was ready to go after him too.

The room began to spin, and I felt like I was in an earthquake, grasping for something solid to hold onto.

A memory of a dream I'd had the previous week suddenly came to mind. I was in a city and there were skyscrapers all around me. I was with several friends, and we were enjoying our time together when suddenly, the sun seemed to disappear and the sky grew dark with clouds, lightning, and rolling thunder. The world seemed to be reeling and spinning, and I told everyone to grab hands and hold on tight. Somehow, I knew that if we held onto each other and embraced the moment, everything would be okay.

Now, in this moment, here in the hospital, I felt the exact same energy and emotions as I had in that dream. The words *embrace the moment* came to me and sent a calming hush through my body, mind, and spirit.

Chris's voice brought me back to reality. He was on the phone with Mike, sharing with him how badly he wanted to punch the doctor. With his phone on speaker, we were all privy to Mike's response, "Well, you do what you need to do, and I'll bring the bail money!"

This had us all laughing and embracing the moment.

The jovial atmosphere helped, but it didn't negate the feelings that ripped through my insides like a train about to jump the tracks. *What if I can never run again?* I shook my head and told myself to embrace the moment and it would all be okay.

The nurse came through with an IV bag filled with fluids to help "quench my thirst."

I really *hate* needles, so the thought of being poked to have the IV drip started didn't thrill me.

Embrace the moment...

I was going to have to have an IV for surgery and this was the beginning of the process.

Attempting to embrace the moment, I explained to the nurse that my veins could be ornery when it came to needles.

She was up for the challenge because one poke of the needle and she was able to get that vein. *Hmm... embrace the moment.*

I could see where my attitude was already helping me, but it sure would have been nice to have some details about this surgery. Like, what exactly happens when they replace your hip? What does that look like? What is the recovery time? How hard is it to "learn to walk" again?

Dr. Charming had not exactly explained anything, so I asked the nurse which doctor would be doing the surgery, praying all the time that the answer was not Dr. Charming.

She took a moment to explain that there was an orthopedic doctor that was already there doing surgery on an elderly woman who had fallen. As soon as he was finished with her, he would be in to see me and go over the details.

Another win, I thought as I continued my attempt to embrace the moment.

The anxiety in the room dropped at this news. I was so relieved, and the rest of the gang seemed to share in my contentment. It was like we had all been holding our breath, and we had just been given the signal that it was okay to breathe again.

Random conversations kept us busy for a couple of hours while, back in Colorado, Mike scurried to pack a duffle bag as well as arrange coverage for both of our businesses in our absence. He had a long drive and a battle with anxiety and regret ahead of him, knowing I was headed for surgery and he was not there.

It was midafternoon when I finally met with my orthopedic surgeon, but it was worth the wait. What an amazing difference! He was a ray of sunshine, literally beaming a radiant smile as he checked in with both Chris and me.

"I hear we have had an exciting day today!" he began, acknowledging that I had been running in the marathon and then listening enthusiastically to the details of my story.

When I was done, he shared what the Xrays had shown and his plan for surgery. But oh... what a different plan!

"Soooo... I doonnn't need a hip replacement?" My voice was shaky.

"Had the break been any further up into the femoral head, you would be looking at hip replacement surgery, for sure," he explained. "However, since the break is at the base of the head, I feel there will be enough blood flow to heal the break."

He continued with additional details of how they would put a rod in my femur and two screws angled through the neck and into the head of the femur to hold it in place, giving it a chance to heal the fracture. A third screw would be placed at the base of the rod to keep everything securely fastened.

"Any questions?" he asked, looking at me with the tenderness of a father for his child. He could tell I was processing all that he had said and patiently waited for my response.

"Will I be able to run again?" I hesitantly asked, preparing myself to embrace the moment, come what may.

His eyes twinkled. "Yes." He paused. "Eventually... You have had quite the injury, and it will take some time to heal. After the surgery, there will be at least six to eight weeks of no more than your big toe touching the ground. No weight on that leg at all. Then another 6-8 months after that, learning to put weight on that leg again and strengthening your muscles, learning to walk before you can even think about running again. And you will have to ease into it, even then." His blue eyes sparkled as he finished, "So to answer your question, Yes, you *will* run again. It's just going to take some time."

Elated, I couldn't help but let out an excited "Whoop, whoop!" My mind calculated the dates, and I figured by late spring, I would be able to start training again. It was a ways down the road, but I had hope.

Embrace the moment.

"Okay then," he chuckled, "The nurse will get you ready for surgery, and I will meet you in the operating room."

"I'm so glad he's my doctor." I reached for Chris's hand and squeezed it reassuringly, feeling confident all would be well.

Embrace the moment.

Before long, they had me prepped and ready to go, fancy backless hospital gown and all. They fixed me a cocktail of anesthesia and wheeled me into the operating room where the only thing I remember was the doctor's blue eyes beaming reassuringly above his mask when he asked me if I was ready.

"Let's do this!" I slurred, smiling groggily, the anesthesia already taking hold.

Swerving Swiftly with a Smile

The surgery took several hours but the next thing I knew, the operation was over and I was waking up in recovery. And oh my... was I nauseous.

Embrace the moment.

In no time at all, they had me up and walking with a walker.

"Want to race?" Chris teased jovially as I began trying to maneuver the walker without putting weight on my leg.

"Maybe next time," I playfully responded, scooting my walker out of the room and into the hallway.

Completing a lap around the nurse's station, I headed back to my bed. I was feeling lightheaded and the queasiness was taking over.

Embrace the moment.

I managed to get myself near the side of the bed and dropped down onto the mattress, with Chris and the nurse assuring me I had done well.

"I feel like I've been run over by a Mack truck," I announced, smiling up at the doctor when he asked me how I was feeling.

"I'm not surprised," he chortled. "You were in surgery for several hours. We did a lot of work on you!"

We talked for a moment and then just before leaving, he caught me off guard when he asked, "Do you have an orthopedic doctor in Colorado that you would prefer to go to?"

A name suddenly came to mind. I had heard good things about this doctor, and it was the best I could come up with.

"You mean...?" and he repeated the name of the doctor, including his first name.

"Yes," I answered, wondering how he knew him.

He proceeded to share with us how they had gone through residency together and then had been part of a research and training program helping injured Navy Seals for several years.

Now that's a "you can't make this story up" moment! What are the odds? And yet... this was the kind of magic that happened as I embraced each obstacle along this journey.

Around 9:45 pm, Mike sped into my room. I'm not sure who was more elated that he was finally there. In a couple of steps, he was by my bedside, leaning over and giving me the biggest hug!

Chris gave his dad the chair and stood talking for a while as I dozed in and out. When I finally woke up, Chris was gone and Mike was lovingly watching me sleep.

"Hello, Sunshine!" he chirped.

"Hey there," I responded sleepily.

That night, Mike slept in the chair. We were coming up on the second anniversary of Mike's dad's passing and here I was, lying in a hospital bed. My heart ached for him. We talked about how hard it was for him to be there, but he didn't want to leave me alone.

He caught a catnap or two, but neither of us really got any sleep. I did several laps around the nurse's station throughout the night and was on the edge of heaving because of the pain medication.

The next day, they kept trying to get me to eat. When the doctor came in, he confirmed I had to eat before they would be able to release me, but the medication was doing a number on me.

Embrace the moment.

"You've got to eat something!" Mike scolded me.

"But I'm not hungry and everything makes me want to throw up," I whined.

"George," he softened, calling me by my nickname. "You have to eat!"

"Only if you want me to puke it all up!" I warned.

I finally managed a couple sips of a protein shake, but no more.

Next time the doctor came by, he burst my bubble when he informed us it would be Monday before they would let me escape the hospital and at least a week before he would release me to go home as they were worried about the long drive, as it put me at a higher risk for blood clots.

Embrace the moment.

It only took being out of the hospital for one day for me to retire the walker and go to crutches. I had discussed this with the doctor before leaving the hospital, and he had given me his blessing but insisted

I be extra careful as I moved in and out of Mike's big four-wheel-drive truck, Chris's apartment nearby, and the hotel we stayed in.

By the time the weekend came, I was going stir crazy!

Embrace the moment.

With Chris's kids in town and Heidi's two, we had plenty of entertainment for the weekend. One day they came over for a swim in the pool and dinner, and the next day we went for a drive to explore some of the mountain roads near Lehi, Utah.

The weather was perfect for checking out the changing colors of the leaves and a picnic together. I was grateful for the kids and their willingness to hang out with me, even though we couldn't do our normal romping and adventuring.

Not to mention I wore down easily.

By the time the weekend was over, I was wiped out and ready to go home. The only thing standing in my way was the doctor's release. My appointment was at 9:30 that next Monday morning and we couldn't wait.

At the appointment, they took a new Xray to see how things were healing. He asked me a few questions and said my doctor back home would like to see me in three to four weeks.

"I have a fitness trainer I work with on Tuesdays and Thursdays," I explained. "Would it be okay to continue with upper body strength training until I can put weight on my leg?"

"Sure. Just don't mess up my good work," he teased as he signed my paperwork.

"I'll behave," I promised.

My instructions were to get out of the truck and *walk* every one to two hours. It would be important for me not to keep my knees bent for too long. Even stretching out in the back seat would be a good idea.

Anything. Just let me go home!

Soon we were on the road to Colorado. I could not wait to be back in my own house and in my own bed, with my own shower, and no more restaurant food.

The seven-hour drive took nearly nine with all the extra stops we had to make. A couple of hours from home, I almost caved and got a hotel, but I again *embraced the moment* and persevered.

I was never so glad to get out of the truck!

I did everything my doctors asked me to do and embraced each moment. Especially the moments of frustration when I felt like I couldn't stand on one foot any longer. I would take a deep breath and reground myself.

Embrace the moment was my mantra, and it made all the difference.

At that four-week check-up, they took an Xray, and the doctor was so impressed with my healing that he released me to start putting weight on my leg, two weeks earlier than predicted.

The doctor in Utah had told me it would take at least six to eight weeks, but I had learned on my last injury go around that kicking against the pricks didn't work and actually caused the healing process to take much longer.

This time I was *embracing the moment*, seeing what was possible instead of what seemed impossible.

Two days later, Joshua asked if I could watch the boys. Only eleven months apart, the youngest was still an infant and the other a toddler. I would have my hands full!

"Sure," I agreed, then added with a laugh, "But let me see if Grammy can help. While I am a master on these crutches, I don't think even I can carry the boys and maneuver the crutches."

Grammy, Mike's mom, agreed to help, and we were having a great day until shortly after naptime. Being over six feet tall, Mike had easily climbed over the baby gate blocking the basement stairs and turned around to tease the toddler sticking his toes between the rails, grabbing at his toes and taunting, "I'm going to get you!"

The little one giggled and was having a great time until Mike's knee went out from under him, and he fell down the stairs, disappearing from sight. The little guy craned his neck to try and find him, and Mike's mom began hollering down the stairs, "Are you okay? Are you okay?" Not waiting for an answer, she was ready to climb over the baby gate. The little ones didn't know what was happening and there I was on crutches trying to bring this circus under control.

Demanding Grammy stop before she climbed over, I made my way to the stairs and took the baby gate down, then started down the stairs with my crutches, instructing Grammy to keep the boys away from the stairs.

Mike finally made it back up the stairs, but he was in a lot of pain.

Attempting to lighten the mood, I teased, "Hey, I know a good orthopedic surgeon."

He just rolled his eyes.

We knew Mike had needed a knee replacement, but his current doctor had been telling him to wait until he absolutely had to.

Mike made an appointment to see my orthopedic surgeon and was scheduled for surgery just a couple of weeks later, on November eleventh.

Embrace the moment.

We were quite the pair of gimps for about six weeks!

My next appointment was the week of Christmas, exactly three months since my injury. The assistant took another Xray and the doctor spent some time showing me the changes from my last appointment to this one.

After he shared his pleasure with my progress, he smiled a big smile. "I don't ever want to see you in here again!"

I was puzzled. "What do you mean?"

"I mean," he started, "I am releasing you, and I don't need to see you again unless you have an unforeseen problem arise."

Of course, you know the question that was on the forefront of my mind! I had to ask.

"So when can I start running?"

He chuckled. "You can start tomorrow if you think you are up to it."

"This is the best Christmas present EVER!" I gave him a big hug.

I'm sure I was beaming from ear to ear as I left his office. I could not wait to let my running buddies know.

Originally, I thought it would be late spring before I could even think about running. Here it was, not even Christmas, and it was a reality.

I am convinced that my positive attitude and mantra gave my body the additional energy to heal. It didn't have to waste healing energy on kicking against the pricks. It spent all its stamina on healing. What an incredible difference.

Feeling the Pain with Power

I contacted my running buddies and several of them met me at the track that next morning. It was a very, *very* slow jog, but I made it an entire mile in spite of the pain.

Probably further than I should have gone, I thought as we finished and everyone gave hugs all around.

I felt like I was going to die by the time I finished but was so elated that I did not want to stop. Even as slow as it was, actually running, after all I had been through…

My mind was filled with joy and my spirit was flying above the clouds as I climbed into the car and drove back home!

But there was another type of pain waiting for me to feel it.

I had worked diligently on my book and had finally finished the process of publishing the first edition on June 30, 2019, six months earlier.

Even with all the work I had done, I'd had so many misgivings! I didn't want to hurt anyone's feelings, especially my dad's. I had struggled for months on whether to continue with the project or let it fall to the wayside.

However, I had made a commitment to God to write this original book. But God would understand, right? I tried to reason that I had done my part and had written the book. Realizing I was trying to bargain my way out of the contract, I had finally determined it had to at least be loaded onto Amazon.

I had set the goal to have it uploaded by July 1, 2019, and as my deadline loomed only hours away, I quickly uploaded it onto Amazon and closed the door on that chapter. I had been as discreet as possible, not telling anyone it was available to purchase. Taking on the mindset that I had done my part of the contract, and the rest was up to God, I had applied all of my energy to my training and the upcoming marathon.

Then the break and the surgery and the recovery. But the deeper pain had begun to surface while I was working through a 21-day writing quest with Amanda.

As I wrote, I realized that I had to reclaim the power I'd given to my dad and his feelings about the book and officially launch it on December 2, 2019, Cyber Monday.

It felt so good to put it out there publicly and receive such amazing feedback, by the time the doctor gave me the green light to run a few months earlier than I planned, I was certain that embracing the moment and taking back my power was definitely the way to change my experience of every single challenge.

But this was only the beginning of taking back my power.

At the end of 2019, Amanda invited me to be part of a collaborative book with her and several of her clients. We were going to meet for a retreat in early 2020 when Covid struck a vicious blow and the world was suddenly turned upside-down, putting everyone on lockdown.

To keep the project moving forward, Amanda decided to hold the retreat online in early March. We all gathered virtually to introduce ourselves and do some get-to-know-you activities.

As the day went on, old, unhealed traumas surfaced from the abuse I had endured as a child, teenager, and a young mother. Deeper layers of feeling unworthy and not good enough surfaced as I listened to these incredible men and women expound on their accomplishments.

What do I possibly have to offer? Feelings of deep insufficiency, overwhelm, and panic overtook me.

When we broke for lunch, I asked Mike if he would go for a short walk with me. Still recuperating from his knee surgery, I knew he could use the walk and I needed both the fresh crisp early spring air and the opportunity to voice my feelings.

Mike had always been my confidant, but I had lost my BFF and advocate to the downward spiral of grief.

He just didn't have the capacity to be my cheerleader in this upcoming adventure.

When he didn't say a lot during that walk, his silence added to my upside-down view of what I had to offer. I kept thinking I might have to back out of the project despite the fact that it would be wholly against my intuition to do so. I wanted to be part of this book project more than anything and was torn between being unable to see what I had to offer and the desire to be part of something incredible.

I couldn't wait to get out of the last session of the day and clicked the "leave meeting" button as quickly as I could, not saying goodbye to anyone for fear the tears that were beginning to form would betray me.

Again, I began a conversation with Mike. This time, his fears struck me like a swift slap in the face.

"You have to give up something or you're going to have a heart attack!" he demanded.

"I am not going to have a heart attack!" I countered angrily. "I just feel inferior to the others on this project." I desperately tried to explain, but his fears escalated.

"You are about to explode!" he snarled and then threatened, "You have to give up something!"

I did not recognize this man. Who was he and where was Mike? The room began to spin, and I felt like I had been catapulted back in time and was facing abusers from the past, being forced to do something I did not want to do.

I wanted to scream, *You can't make me!*

Instead, I angrily enquired, "And just what would you like me to give up?" and proceeded to list off the larger items that were on my very full plate.

"I cannot stop running the office! That is our livelihood!"

Mike grumbled inaudibly as I presented the second option.

"And I am not going to tell Heavenly Father that I am too busy to do what he has asked me to do as Relief Society president!"

"Well, you have to give up something!" he spat back.

Taking a deep breath and lowering my voice to nearly a whisper, "The only thing left for me to give up is my writing."

"Then give it up!" he demanded.

I didn't know what to do. I was stunned, hurt, and feeling desperately alone.

Who was this person? This was so out of character for the man I knew and loved. I had never seen him like this, and yet I couldn't think about him. I had not felt this violated since before my divorce.

Seeing him spinning through all his own anxiety and overwhelm, I felt trapped. I loved Mike deeply and didn't want to send him toppling any further over the edge.

So, I fell back into the old story of worrying about others before taking care of myself.

"Fine..." I replied, sounding like a hurt puppy.

"Fine!" he snapped with glazed over eyes.

I had already turned in my rough draft of the project to Amanda, so I wasn't terribly concerned and hoped the backlash from this outburst would soon pass.

However, with Covid came masks, which was just another source of anxiety from the trauma I had faced from abusers. Swearing not to break my promise, I had no way to process these emotions. Journaling was writing, so the emotions just kept piling up and up as I desperately tried to swerve around each of the roadblocks and obstacles on my path!

For the next nine months, there were no retreats or quests, or much community activity in the writing group. Of course, it didn't matter because I would have been breaking my oath if I got involved. Thank goodness my leg had healed enough that I was hiking quite a bit and running again.

I had a goal to run a half-marathon on my one-year anniversary of the femur break. This goal became my focus and my only source of enjoyment and grounding as I met with running buddies to work out at the track and other local trails.

Early in December, Mike cornered me one morning. "What's going on?"

We hadn't had a real conversation in months. In fact, I could hardly stand to be in the same room with him.

"What do you mean?" I countered, feeling threatened by his question.

"Why don't your eyes light up anymore when I walk into the room?"

This caught me off-guard and I didn't have a good answer for him, so I gave him a noncommittal shrug. "I don't know."

However, his question started me thinking about how miserable, angry, and emotionally spent I was whenever I was near him. I found great joy as I trained and reached my goal to run that half-marathon or spent time hiking or running in every other free moment I could muster. It was the only time I felt alive.

I realized I was furious at him for turning his desperation from his dad's passing into a battle against me. And I was furious at myself for allowing another man to manipulate me emotionally and cross that boundary I had set a long time ago.

I was not sure we would be able to work through this and seriously started thinking about what my options were.

Then, on Christmas day, Mike started in again, "Why is it that your eyes don't light up when I enter the room?"

Here we go again.

"What are you talking about?" I feigned ignorance. It was Christmas Day and I really didn't want to go down this rabbit hole.

"The only time I see your eyes light up is when you are with your running or hiking friends. They never light up for me. I don't understand?"

I was incredulous. You could almost hear an audible crack, as if a lightning bolt had struck nearby. I had reached my limit and was ready to take back my power.

"Really?" I lashed out and moved closer to where he was sitting. "It couldn't be because you told me I had to stop the one thing that brings me joy?"

Looking at me as if I was speaking a foreign language, he snapped, "What are you talking about?"

"My writing!" I spat.

"I never told you that you couldn't write!" he defended.

"Oh... Whoa... Just one minute," he sounded like my narcissistic father gaslighting me, so I reminded him of the ultimatum he gave me.

"I never meant it that way," he began, but I cut him off before he could spew anything further.

It was the first time in nearly a year that we had really had a conversation. Emotional roller coaster doesn't even begin to describe the next couple of hours. However, by the time it was over, we had both agreed that we loved each other deeply and our relationship was worth fighting for. We promised to put forth our best efforts while, together, we slogged through the minutia of feelings and worked on falling in love all over again.

Triage and Healing in Community

Opportunities to slow down, swerve, and feel the pain seem to be never-ending. There were many things that transpired over the next several years, each obstacle with its own challenges to triage and heal.

One of the areas where I found healing came in July of 2022 while working on generational trauma. For the first time ever, I found myself viewing my dad in a different light.

There were a couple of people in our writing community that had read a book on generational trauma. They had great results healing some of their old stories, so I bought two copies, one for me and one for someone I knew that was struggling with similar challenges.

The day it arrived, I opened it and began reading the first chapter. About four pages in, my stomach began turning flip-flops and things seemed hazy and unclear.

What the heck? I put the book aside. *Maybe tomorrow.*

Over the next several months, each time I attempted to read this book, my mind would go foggy and my stomach would roll, leading me to leave it for another day until finally, in frustration, I declared, "This is ridiculous!" as I slammed the book shut again and stuck it on the shelf for over a year.

In January of 2023, I made a pact with another writer to read it and meet up over Zoom to discuss the current chapter. However, we were never able to make it happen.

Still not ready...

In April of 2023, I was headed to a retreat and several of us were on our Tuesday check-in call when the subject of this book came up again. Mike and I had sold our house earlier that year and moved into our camper full-time so all of my books, including this one, were packed away in storage.

No way... It can't be true, I thought as I remembered that I had placed the second copy of the book in a pocket behind the driver's seat of my car when I first bought it so I would have it the next time I saw that acquaintance, and it was still there.

Hmm... Was it really for her? I think not.

I told the group about the book being in my car adding, "You just can't make this stuff up! Guess that means I need to give it another try."

When I arrived at the retreat, I grabbed the book out of its hiding place and began the process of reading again. This time, I didn't experience any of the fog or nausea.

Then in July, while doing some of the homework in the book, I had an epiphany. I came to the realization that I really didn't know what my dad had experienced growing up. Even though my sister and I had spent time with our grandparents for two weeks during many of our summers as kids, I really didn't know anything about Dad's childhood or what kind of traumas he had experienced, with one exception of a profound loss of a loved one with no opportunity to say goodbye.

I have also come to believe my dad has undiagnosed bipolar disorder. These two things alone were enough to change my story about the man who had raised me and abused me.

Dad had struggles and conflicts of his own growing up. He was just a man, doing the best he could, with the limited tools and knowledge he possessed.

This realization completely changed the feelings I had been carrying around for decades.

Witnessing him in this light, I found grace and forgiveness that would have been impossible before. Relinquishing a ton of baggage in our relationship allowed me to truly love him for who he is and to stop being angry at him for not being who I thought he should be.

It was a turning point that allowed me to have the capacity the following month to take over as Power of Attorney for him as the Alzheimer's continues to take his mind and he slips further and further away.

This was life-changing, but even larger transformations were on the horizon.

While attending Amanda's story-healing retreat in January 2023, I realized that so many of the challenges I was facing revolved around my discomfort with vulnerability. Not just on a personal level with Mike, but in many other relationships, including business, family, friends, church. You name it. They all seemed to be entangled and intertwined and vulnerability was the key to unraveling them.

Now what I am about to say may sound crazy, but I am telling you, it was the best medicine for this nearly sixty-year-old soul. The fix I found was as simple and yet complex as renegotiating a new relationship with vulnerability.

I told you it was a crazy idea! But it worked. I felt all the feels while writing out the new terms of our relationship. Anger, frustration, exhaustion, regret, shame, insufficiency, and lack of lovability, along with more than a tinge of excitement at the possibility of rewriting this destructive pattern.

When I had the final draft of the new contract written, I called Mike and asked him if he would be willing to read through it with me. Our relationship had steadily improved, and I wanted his reaction to the new relationship and to see if he saw anything I had missed.

Even though our love was stronger than before, I intended to find out if Mike felt he had healed enough that he could be my cheerleader and support, especially during those negative moments when my ability to conquer a particular obstacle might meet with this old destructive pattern. Could he help me through the process of changing those neuropathways when I needed him most? I wasn't sure I wanted to tackle anything this big without my best friend and champion supporter.

Mike loved the idea of the new relationship with vulnerability and gave me his full support as I moved through the nightmares, abuse, and shame of the past; learned to set even tighter and truer boundaries for myself and others; and cleared out that mental and emotional clutter that was holding me back in so many ways.

We had become avid communicators. As soon as there was any tension on either side, we checked in with each other's feelings and thoughts. As he helped me with this new experience with vulnerability, this honest communication became our barometer that kept us from falling back down the rabbit hole of fear.

I soon learned that vulnerability had many aspects, one of the largest being the ability to set boundaries with those around me. The struggle was real and still wrapped up in those old stories of not being good enough. Especially when I found myself in the midst of a confrontation with family, those old emotions around my lack of worth along with fear and anxiety that they would no longer love me raced along those old neuropathways like race cars around the Indy 500.

I hated being confrontational and, prior to my contract with vulnerability, would find myself caving in yet again, which in the aftermath left me feeling angry and frustrated for allowing myself to be manipulated and used yet again.

This *had* to change, and change it did.

Soon after that January retreat, I grabbed vulnerability by the hand and took some pretty incredible risks with several people, including family, friends, and employees. I drew a line in the sand and set firmly defined boundaries for all.

Using kindness and love to set boundaries was key for me. I still do not like confrontation, but I hate being manipulated even more. Finding ways to present my boundaries that left no room for argument was essential. When others did not see things my way, I would say, "I'm sorry you feel that way," with each attempt to drag me into a battle until they realized I was not going to argue.

Some, when they realized I couldn't be swayed, would try to manipulate and destroy me and my integrity in other malicious and vindictive manners, showing their true colors and intentions. When even this did not cause me to cave, they would eventually stomp off, grumbling as they left.

The rest, those who truly cared about me, ultimately gained a new respect for me and some showed they loved me even more. Even when they didn't necessarily like the boundaries I had set, they eventually understood that I had made a stand and was not going to budge.

Being vulnerable allowed me to take back my power and stand tall, knowing that I deserved to be loved and respected, not manipulated and used. Rewiring those old stories and writing new ones also helped me develop this new superpower. Learning to set boundaries has forever altered the way I see myself and my relationship with others.

Momentum for More than Me

The good news is that as we create new and improved pathways of healing, additional trails of adventure and growth rise to the surface. It's not always easy. In fact, sometimes it's downright painful, but I have empowered myself with new tools and one of the biggest realizations and gifts of this journey is that I don't have to do it myself.

I have cultivated relationships with different people to support me in a variety of capacities. Mike has stepped back into being my BFF and cheerleader, and I am his.

Amanda, as always, is constantly pushing me to my limits of what I think I can do and then insisting I go one step further. I am eternally grateful for her "gentle nudges."

I count on my dear mentor and friend LeeAnn for all my running, biking, and as of this past year triathlon adventures. She is always there encouraging, supporting, and sharing her experience to help me with mine.

Then there are other friends and family that have taken what I have learned and are now applying it to their lives in small and large ways. It is so exciting to see them heal wounds of their own as we support each other along this healing journey.

The more tools we can obtain and use constructively, the more we can change and improve our life and positively impact the lives of those around us.

My passion has always been to help others. Since writing the first edition of this book, I've remembered a longstanding desire to write a children's book and am dedicated to making a difference for all children and how they see the world.

As grandchildren came along, my desire to create change began as play dates with my youngest two granddaughters when they were both just a few months old. As they grew and we added more grandchildren, this evolved into cousin camps, hiking, scuba training and trips, and other special adventures where I crafted opportunities to help them see the world from a different perspective, giving them tools at a young age that I didn't even begin to acquire until I was nearly fifty years old.

Imagine what could be possible if we introduced our young children, grandchildren, nieces, nephews, and all the other littles in our lives to the tools that will help them maneuver through the inevitable challenges of life more freely and fiercely.

My momentum has been building as I've been considering these possibilities and particularly when I partnered with a few of my magical friends to launch Saved By Story Publishing!

Coupled with my passion to make this world a better place, I have decided to create a series of children's books that are going to be fun and give kids just the tools they need.

The first one is an adapted retelling of a few of my personal Mima adventures with my three oldest granddaughters, when they were between the ages of five and eight.

These books will be great read-together stories for five- and six-year-olds as well as fun beginning chapter books for those seven to ten, helping them to see how they, too, can do hard things and embrace the moment, and that they are stronger than they think they are.

Of course, the momentum isn't confined to my creativity.

Mike and I recently decided it was time to invite others to manage our business, so we can enjoy some adventures together.

And I'm still running...

After completing a virtual half-marathon during the lockdown in 2020 to celebrate my one-year recovery, I decided to run one of the half-marathons just outside of St. George and took third place in my age group.

After that race, I wanted to know if I could run a marathon or if it would be too much. I didn't want to risk another injury, but I was feeling so good that I made an appointment with my doctor in Colorado for the end of March and requested an Xray.

When the doctor came in, he pulled up my current Xray and the one from fifteen months earlier when he had released me to begin running.

"What brings you back in?" the doctor queried.

"I would like to run a marathon, but I want to make sure that my leg still looks good and that I am not going to do more damage to it by running the longer distances."

He took a longer look at my Xrays. "You want to run a marathon, so what have you been doing?"

I explained how I had trained and ran the virtual half-marathon on my one-year anniversary and that I had just run a second race in January and finished in third place.

Pointing, he showed the fracture line where the break had happened on the previous Xray, but on the current one, there was no fracture line to be found.

"This bone is probably the strongest bone in your body," he remarked. "You will have no problems running the distance on it."

I couldn't have been happier and began preparing to run the Huntsville marathon that September. I did a lot of hiking and biking as well as running, as I prepared to meet that mountain again.

On September 18, 2021, I completed my second marathon and set a new personal record.

I ran the Ogden marathon in May of 2022, hiked Longs Peak in August, and then ran my first ultra-marathon in September, completing thirty-two miles and five thousand feet of elevation to finish the race. I ended the year with a half-marathon in October while mentoring a friend on her first half-marathon adventure.

In July of 2023, for my sixtieth birthday present to myself, I checked another first off my bucket list when I gathered all of the kids and grandkids and we all ventured out to one of the municipal airports nearby. Mike and the grandkids watched as Chris, Heidi, and I went up in a plane and proceeded to jump out of that perfectly good airplane. Skydiving was my way of showing my family, especially the grandkids, that you are never too old to try something new.

In August, I found myself running another relay adventure called the Wild West Relay, stepping out of my comfort zone, as I had joined an entirely new group of people for this race. It was such a great experience that I did it again in 2024 and am preparing to run it for the third time in 2025.

In September, I ran the ultra race for a second time. Finding that running the longer distances without months of intense training was hard on the body, I ended the year with another challenge and began training for my first sprint triathlon in February 2024.

Due to an abundance of rain in Southern California and high bacteria levels, they had to remove the swim portion of this race and made it a run, bike, run. I was both disappointed and relieved as I felt the need for more training to really do well in the swim portion. However, I discovered I have a great love for biking and want to do even more. What a win!

Not to be discouraged, I continued training for another sprint triathlon event held in June 2024, this time completing the swim, bike, and running events. My goal for years has been to run a marathon on my ninetieth birthday, but you never know, I may decide I like these multi-event races even more.

What I have discovered to be true is that each time I challenge myself to a new goal, whether that be a new sport event or a new relationship with vulnerability and others, I stretch and grow and become more of what I was put here on earth to be.

Now, what about you? What are the adventures or challenges that interest you or that have come to mind as you have read my story? What's on your bucket list? What will encourage you to take a leap of faith, believe in yourself, and try something you have always wanted to do?

A Special Invitation

TAKING OUR CHILDREN ON ADVENTURES

If you have enjoyed *A Moment in Time* and learning new tools here, please check out my Cousin Camp Chronicles series for kids.

Imagine giving a child tools that can help them slow down and evaluate situations, swerve around the potholes so many fall into, feel the pain and embrace the moments, then triage and heal through story, and build momentum with tools for a lifetime of healthy awareness and healing.

Scan the QR Code below to get a sneak peek of the first book *The Ascent* today!

About

LORI GIESEY

When a serious car accident devastated her life as a happy and active wife, mother, and leader in her community, Lori Giesey chose to fight back. She chose surgery over doctors' incorrect diagnosis, and full recovery over their limiting post-surgery prognosis. She even chose facing off with the voices from her past that told her she wasn't good enough, strong enough, or worthy of being whole and healthy again. Relentless in her pursuit to reclaim "the real Lori" and experience her true potential, she chose to embark on the adventure of her life—and stay on it, even when the terrain got rough. Within a few years, she was a business owner again, a regular half-marathon runner, a high-adventurer, and a writer—enjoying life with her family.

Over the years, Lori has held various leadership roles with adults and youth. She worked with young women to create "Girl's Camp" adventures for nearly two decades; and in the past ten years, she has enjoyed creating and participating in high-adventure team opportunities where individuals learn that the choice to create and live your own highest adventure is a lot easier and a lot more fun and rewarding than just letting life happen to you.

Today, as partner at Saved By Story Publishing, Lori is helping others to write and share their stories while publishing a series of children's books of her own titled Cousin Camp Chronicles. Of course, she's still enjoying new adventures of participating in marathon, ultra-marathon, and triathlon races.

Through all of her writing and adventures, Lori continues to inspire and empower both young and old to reach higher, go further, and become more than they ever imagined.

Lori loves traveling with her husband and best friend, Mike, and they have recently found their perfect spot in the Black Hills of South Dakota where they are creating their own special family haven.